THE WILEY/INSTITUTE OF MANAGEMENT ACCOUNTANTS PROFESSIONAL BOOK SERIES

ACCOUNTING FOR FIXED ASSETS

RAYMOND H. PETERSON

JOHN WILEY & SONS, INC.

New York • Chichester • Brisbane • Toronto • Singapore

Library of Congress Cataloging-in-Publication Data:
Peterson, Raymond H., 1938–
    Accounting for fixed assets / Raymond H. Peterson.
        p.   cm. — (The Wiley Institute of Management Accountants
professional book series)
    ISBN 0-471-53703-9
    1. Capital—Accounting. 2. Assets (Accounting) I. Title.
II. Series.
HF5681.C25P48   1994
657'.73—dc20   93-9023
Printed in the United States of America

10 9 8 7 6 5 4 3 2 1

DEDICATION

To a number of people who influenced my life and prepared me for the job of creating this book:

First, my mother, who not only taught me to read, but allowed me to experience the enjoyment of reading. She opened up for me the vast knowledge available in libraries.

Dr. Wade Moorehouse, retired Professor of Accounting and former Chairman of the Department of Business and Economics at California State University, Hayward, who many years ago, when I was an undergraduate student in his accounting course, stimulated my excitement about the accounting function. Blessed with classes of fewer than six students in a new university, we spent many class hours discussing the theory of accounting. These discussions had a large impact on my career direction.

Earl Malone, a District Accounting Manager, who early in my career forced me to develop my own thoughts and not just rely on past practice. He also taught me the skill of dictation, which made the creation of this book a possibility.

Dodie, world's best secretary, who converted my ramblings into a manuscript.

I wish to thank my wife and best friend, Ettamarie, for putting up with my years of getting this book together. She never tired of asking "how's the book coming?" Her faith that I would finish the task kept me going.

I accept all responsibility for the content; I should, however, recognize the review and suggestions of Alfred King, of IMA, Senior Vice President Valuation Research Corporation and Dr. Anheney Campbell, Accounting Professor, California State University, Turlock.

CONTENTS

ABOUT THE AUTHOR

Raymond (Ray) H. Peterson is currently the senior partner of Ray Peterson & Associates, a consulting firm offering business assistance in establishing and changing accounting systems. He also serves as treasurer of a number of nonprofit organizations. He has over thirty years experience as a management accountant with the Bell System. He retired as Director of Financial Accounting with Pacific Bell.

Mr. Peterson has managed the design of Pacific Telephone and Telegraph Companies detail property records. During the three-year breakup of the Bell System, he was appointed to a Federal Communications Commission task force to create a new uniform system of accounts for telephone companies. The proposed system was adopted by the FCC and was installed in all telephone companies.

Mr. Peterson is a member of the Institute of Management Accountants' Subcommittee on Management Accounting Statement Promulgation. He received a BS from California State University at Hayward and an MBA from Golden Gate University in San Francisco. He also taught accounting and management information systems at Golden Gate University.

PREFACE

This book is designed for accountants and managers who want to get the most from the physical assets of their organizations.

Most readers are already familiar with the concepts and practical application of total quality management (TQM), zero defects, and the other procedures that describe a continued process of improvement. Having made the process and management changes that brought about easy improvements in quality and cost reduction, they are ready to answer the following questions:

How are you applying the principles of continuous improvement to the management of property, plant, and equipment?

Do you have a process in place that allows you to monitor the status of maintenance (or deferred maintenance) on your property, plant, and equipment?

What is the age of the oldest piece of your production equipment?

Do you have a plan in place for replacement of production facilities?

Are there any quality problems in your production or service delivery system caused by property, plant, and equipment failures?

What is the utilization percentage of the property, plant, and equipment?

Can you determine the utilization of your most expensive piece of equipment?

Do you have service or production problems attributable to equipment not being available at the place needed?

Are all of your property, plant, and equipment being utilized to their fullest?

Do you have in place a process that monitors the current condition, evaluates the future need for replacement, and brings to your attention needs to modify that plan?

Do you manage your physical assets or do you put them in place, use them and replace them when they are worn out?

Do your plans include having the necessary cash to purchase replacement physical assets or will you have to do an extraordinary financing or fund-raising when you are surprised by their failure?

Is there a plan in place for overall management or do you simply hope your assets will continue to allow you to produce your product or provide your service?

The purpose of providing this book on accounting for property, plant, and equipment, is to provide the framework for you to install in your organization accounting processes and procedures that will allow you to manage long-term physical assets.

How can a book on assets help answer these questions? All accounting students learn the basics about assets within various accounting courses, however, there really is not much definitive information available on fixed assets in the accounting literature. The Accounting Principles Board and the Financial Accounting Standards Board are both silent on the subject of accounting standards for fixed assets. Lacking a primary source for accounting standards, it is necessary to look to secondary sources, which also contain very little information on the handling of assets. Most accounting textbooks devote only a single chapter to capitalization of assets, and do not cover the subject in depth. Accounting periodicals have focused on valuation of assets, but offer little on specific concepts of capitalization. The issue of valuing at historical cost versus current market price has received considerable interest over the years.

A number of organizations including the American Institute of Certified Public Accountants, the Institute of Management Accountants, and the Government Finance Officers Association offer courses on capitalization of assets. Most of these courses, however, cover either the tax implications of assets or the valuation question. Little in these courses describes how to establish asset policies, document them in a manual, and apply them within the company.

During 1989–90, the National Association of Accountants (now the Institute of Management Accountants) replaced their original Statement on Management Accounting (SMA) on Fixed Assets with two statements relating to accounting for property, plant, and equipment. *SMA 4J,** published in 1989, described the accounting for property, plant, and equipment, and *SMA 4L,*** published in 1990, covers control of property, plant, and equipment. A research issues publication called the *Reporting, Control, and Analysis of Property, Plant, and Equipment* was published in 1990. This collection of publications represents the majority of the available information on accounting for fixed assets as a part of the IMA team coordinating those projects. I became convinced this book was needed.

There is a need to emphasize that assets must be managed, not just purchased, used up, and replaced. The objective is to provide not only accounting for assets, but include that accounting in a process that will allow management to get the most out of the company's investment. It is not always possible to create more debt in order to acquire assets. Therefore, some of our consumption must be sacrificed today in order to provide quality assets for tomorrow.

In today's complex business best quality and maximum utilization are going to give the best return on investment. *Accounting for Fixed Assets* contains more than the routine accounting processes. It also has the management framework that must surround the accounting process.

The United States economy has been built since World War II as "a paper plate society." We rapidly built our economy based on the philosophy of quick production without much concern for quality. We built automobiles that only lasted a few years, and, in fact, are still building houses in the same way that we did in the early 1950s. They require major renovation every fifteen to twenty years. Many of the houses of the early 1950s are currently the subject of redevelopment districts: they either require major repair or must be ripped out and replaced. We have built a tremendous economy and brought the majority of citizens to the highest standard of living of any culture with this "do-it-quick" philosophy. It created many jobs, especially at the unskilled and semiskilled level, and brought the pleasure of accomplishment and the fruits of labor to the largest segment of U.S. citizens quickly. We have done so, however, for the sake of today and at the expense of tomorrow. But tomorrow has arrived, and we cannot continue to use up our assets. Those assets capable of bringing future benefits must be managed in a way that will allow those future benefits to occur.

The European and Japanese economies have grown much more slowly; jobs and the rewards that come from labors are just now reaching many segments of those cultures. However, the infrastructure base there, the assets like roads, houses, and other buildings, constructed in the 1950s is still in use and not in need of major repairs. A complete difference in philosophical approach was used in building the base for their economies. They have not sacrificed tomorrow for today, but in fact sacrificed yesterday for today—and today has arrived.

Assets are those things we purchase today that will bring future benefits. But those assets must be managed to get those future benefits. To compete in a level playing field across the world, instead of in one where we make all the rules, we in the United States must evaluate our present practices. We can no longer afford to put two or three times the percentage of our gross national product into the nation's dumps each year than competing countries do. We can no longer approach the building and operating of our businesses as we did during World War II. We learned there that we can build things quickly if they are only needed for a few years or are abandoned on the battle field. Much of our managerial approach to business assets is alarmingly similar: build it, use it, and throw it away. To many, it is even worse than that; we buy it and don't think about it again until it is worn out or disrupts the production line.

Accounting managers must rethink their accounting processes for assets. To be value-added, accounting information must be simple and understandable, and must provide relevant, timely information to those who make decisions based on it.

My goal in producing this book is not just to provide a comprehensive treatment of the details of accounting for fixed assets, but also to provide the management accountant with the processes to provide good relevant decision-making information for the officers of the company. Also, I provide the processes that are necessary to manage those assets.

The book is organized to allow you to skip over the initial processes necessary to the system, and understand the principals and philosophy that are necessary in managing assets.

I will also suggest a different approach to management of assets. An asset is current production that is not used up, and instead provides the means for future productivity. A hundred years ago, assets were known by business people as capital goods. Capital goods are something that must be managed for the future, not just to benefit current quarter earnings.

1

WHAT IS ACCOUNTING FOR FIXED ASSETS?

INTRODUCTION

Most accounting professionals believe that all there is to be learned about asset accounting occurred in the introductory course on principles of accounting. Therefore, although this subject can become quite complex, yet it is explored in very little of the accounting literature.

In 1984 when the Federal Communications Commission (FCC) called for the rewriting of the uniform system of accounts for telephone companies, public utilities had not been following generally accepted accounting principles (GAAP) as outlined by the Financial Accounting Standards Board (FASB) and its predecessors, but instead used procedures that had been outlined in 1934 by the FCC. The team responsible for making recommendations on the rewriting of the system of accounts established a basic policy that what was to be recommended would comply with current GAAP.

The subcommittee responsible for reviewing and recommending procedures for property, plant, and equipment was frustrated by the lack of definitive information on accounting for assets. The primary sources are very limited. The Accounting Principles Board (APB) and the later Financial Accounting Standards Board have been nearly silent on the subject beyond defining depreciation and historical costs.

Accounting Research Bulletin (ARB) 43 was issued in 1953 to summarize all previous GAAP. It requires that depreciation be calculated and disclosed. Most of the additional discussion on tangible

1

assets involved explaining why depreciation is appropriately calculated using historical costs. It is true that management must take into consideration the probability that plant and machinery will have to be replaced at cost much greater than those of the facilities now in use; however, depreciation must not be calculated on the basis of this expected inflation.

ARB 43 in paragraph C5 goes on to state:

> The cost of a reproductive facility is one of the costs of the services it renders during its useful economic life. Generally accepted accounting principles require that this cost be spread over the expected useful life of the facility in such a way as to allocate it as equitably as possible to the periods during which services are obtained from the use of the facility. This procedure is known as depreciation accounting, a system of accounting which aims to distribute the cost or other basic value of tangible capital assets, less salvage (if any), over the estimated useful life of the unit (which may be a group of assets) in a systematic and rational matter. It is a process of allocation, not of valuation.

After formation of the Accounting Principles Board, *APB 6* was issued in 1964 continuing the authority outlined in *ARB 43*. The Board continued to support the use of historical cost as opposed to inflation accounting:

The Board is of the opinion that property, plant, and equipment should not be written up by an entity to reflect appraisal, market or current values which are above cost to the entity.

APB 12, issued in 1967, requires the disclosure of depreciable assets and depreciation. In addition to total depreciation expense and the major classes of depreciable assets, it also requires disclosure of:

A. Depreciation expense for the period.

B. Balances of major classes of depreciable assets by nature of function, at the balance sheet date.

C. Accumulated depreciation, either by major classes of depreciable assets or in total, at the balance sheet date.

D. A general description of the method or methods used in computing depreciation with respect to major classes of depreciable assets.

CONSUMPTION OF BENEFITS

In 1984, the Financial Accounting Standards Board issued *Concept Statement 5*, which included additional discussion of assets. However, it was also limited in scope, as one would expect in a concept statement.

The discussion emphasized the recognition assumption of assets, clearly indicating that assets are consumed by their use and the cost, should be recognized in the accounting periods of their life.

Consumption of economic benefits during a period may be recognized either directly or by relating it to revenues recognized during the period.

Some expenses such as depreciation and insurance are allocated by systematic and rational procedures to the period during which the related assets are expected to provide benefits.

"Any expense or loss (in future benefits) is recognized if it becomes evident that previously recognized future economic benefits of an asset have been reduced or eliminated."

Since its creation, the Financial Accounting Standards Board has entertained considerable discussion about assets, but the only statements issued cover specific assets:

- Expensing versus capitalizing research and development
- The accounting for software
- Including depreciation in not-for-profit organization financial statements

FASB Concept Statement 6, Elements of Financial Statements, has more material than any other on the accounting for long-term tangible assets. However, it addresses itself primarily to the definition, the purpose of accrual accounting, and the characteristics of an asset.

In 1985, *Concept Statement 6* added a definition of assets:

"Assets are probable future economic benefits obtained or controlled by a particular entity as a result of past transactions or events."

3

CHARACTERISTICS OF ASSETS

Concept Statement 6 continues, enumerating the three essential characteristics of an asset:

A. It embodies a probable future benefit that involves a capacity, singly or in combination with other assets, to combine directly or indirectly to future net cash in flows,

B. A particular entity can obtain the benefit and control others' access to it.

C. The transaction or other event giving rise to the entity's right to or control of the benefit has already occurred.

This is the first discussion in promulgated accounting rules discussing the definition and characteristics of an asset. The major thrust is that probable future benefit is the definition of an asset. In order to reflect it on the balance sheet, the entity must be able to obtain benefit from the asset and control others' access to the asset. This statement also reviews the concept of future economic benefit and service potential as it relates to not-for-profit organizations. It states:

> In a not-for-profit organization, the service potential or future economic benefit is used to provide desired or needed goods or services to beneficiaries or other constituents, which may or may not directly result in net cash inflows to the organizations. Some not-for-profit organizations rely significantly on contributions or donations of cash to supplement selling prices. . . .

This discussion introduces the argument that depreciation of tangible assets is an appropriate expense of not-for-profit organizations.

In a discussion of accrual accounting, *Concept Statement 6* discusses assets under a heading "Recognition, Matching, and Allocation." In paragraph 145, it states:

> Accrual accounting uses accrual, deferral, and allocation procedures whose goal is to relate revenues, expenses, gains, and losses to periods to reflect an entity's performance during a period instead of merely listing its cash receipts and outlays . . . the goal of accrual accounting is to

account in the periods in which they occur for the effects on an entity of transactions and other events and circumstances, to the extent that those financial effects are recognizable and measurable.

There is a discussion of costs and revenues to determine profits for periods. Depreciation and assets are excluded from the matching concept. Paragraph 149 of *Concept Statement 6* explains:

> However, many assets yield their benefit to an entity over several periods, for example, prepaid insurance, buildings, and various kinds of equipment. Expenses resulting from their use are normally allocated to the periods of the estimated useful lives (the periods over which they are expected to provide benefits) by a rational allocation procedure, for example, by recognizing depreciation or other amortization. Although the purpose of expense allocation is the same as that of other expense recognition—to reflect the using up of assets as a result of transactions or other events or circumstances affecting an entity—allocation is applied if causal relations are generally, but not specifically, identified. For example, wear and tear from use is known to be a major cause of the expense called depreciation, but the amount of depreciation caused by wear and tear in a period normally cannot be measured.

This discussion appears to make the distinction between the matching principle for revenues and expenses and the allocation of the cost of using up future benefits. Although this distinction is subtle, it is the point of basic disagreement between those who argue for inflation accounting and the depreciating of assets based on current market value and those who argue for depreciating using a lesser historical cost.

Appendix B of *Concept Statement 6* further discusses characteristics of assets, defining assets as "probable future economic benefits obtained or controlled by a particular entity as a result of past transactions or events."

Most of this discussion relates to non-tangible or non-physical assets. The Financial Accounting Standards Board, in issuing its *Statement 2, Accounting for Research and Development Costs*, also gives us some information on what makes up tangible physical assets. In their concern for the appropriate accounting for research and development costs, they conclude that all should be charged to expense accounts. However, they do give us their thoughts about which tangible assets should and should not be included in research and development costs.

A prime consideration is that materials, equipment, and facilities that have an alternative future use (in research and development projects or otherwise) shall be capitalized as tangible assets when acquired or constructed. However, the costs of such materials, equipment, or facilities that are acquired or constructed for a particular research and development project and have no alternative future uses and therefore no separate economic values are research and development costs at the time the costs are incurred. All research and development costs encompassed by the statement are charged to expense when incurred. This reflects the concept that research and development costs will be used up during the span of the research project. However, tangible assets that have a life beyond the current project should be capitalized and depreciated over their useful lives.

The preceding paragraphs summarize the present state of GAAP relating to property, plant, and equipment.

Many subjects in accounting have not been covered at length within the promulgated statements. Most with the significance of long-term tangible assets have been covered in more detail in secondary accounting material. However, few secondary publications provide any in-depth discussion on fixed assets.

Research bulletins and disclosure drafts having to do with inflation accounting have not been allowed to creep into generally accepted accounting principles.

Therefore, in determining the details of an accounting system for property, plant, and equipment with the FCC study in 1984 and 1985, the committee felt it necessary to use the secondary documents on assets. The documents were used to establish current practice and to form a model that telecommunications companies should use instead of the 1934 FCC regulations. The only additional definitive document discussing accounting for property, plant, and equipment was issued by the Institute on Management Accounting (IMA, formerly the National Association of Accountants) as *Statement on Management Accounting (SMA) 4. SMA 4* was issued in October, 1972 with the title *Fixed Asset Accounting: The Capitalization of Cost.* A number of concepts are discussed in this twenty-four-page statement.

Concepts outlined in SMA 4 include:

Costs through preparation for use

Extraordinary repairs

Base unit

Extended life or increased capacity

Written policies

Capitalization policy

Life greater than one year

Self-constructed assets that include direct overhead

No initial development cost

Depreciation

This statement discusses a number of concepts which were then, and still are, common practice.

All Costs to Prepare Item for Use

All costs in addition to the invoice price to make an item of property, plant, and equipment ready for use should be capitalized in its historical cost.

Extraordinary Repairs

Normal repairs are charged to expense when incurred; however, extraordinary repairs that extend the life, increase the capability, or increase efficiency of the item should be capitalized during its life, the historical cost increased, and depreciation recalculated from that date on.

Base Unit

This concept is not dealt with in any other document. It outlines the concept that property units should have a policy determination as to what constitutes the property record entity that is capitalized. It might be a complete machine or the base unit may be the individual components of that machine. This is an important concept in order to establish a usable property record system for a particular company. For example, entities that use light trucks as maintenance vehicles may wear out a number of trucks during the lives of hydraulic lifts, welding equipment, and utility beds.

Written Policies

It is important for each company to have an asset manual with written policies. Determinations of appropriate base units and other policies unique to a company need to be described and documented. Without written policies, asset accounting will not be consistent over a period of time.

Capitalization Policy

A minimum level of capitalization should be identified. Accounting records that cost more than the items are worth are not cost effective.

Life Greater than One Year

Policy should emphasize that items with a life restricted to one accounting period should be expensed no matter what their cost.

Self-Constructed Assets

All costs of preparing assets for use should be capitalized. However, only directly attributable or traceable overhead costs should be included. General and administrative overhead costs should not be capitalized. If a company is not in the business of constructing assets, overhead costs are not likely to be increased by an individual construction project. Therefore, if those costs were capitalized, expenses in the accounting period that the asset was being constructed would be improperly reduced. Additionally, the initial development cost of making a decision on which project to construct should not be included in capitalizable costs. Subsequent costs for a specific project, once the decision has been made, are capitalized.

Depreciation

The idea of the relative permanence of assets that are "fixed" is questioned by *SMA 4*. The statement notes that periods of nonuse should be excluded from the depreciation schedule: "Until these assets can be said to have completely satisfied the purpose for which they are intended—normal or acceptable production capability—they are, for the time being, suspended accounting-wise in a sort of hiatus, not producing income, hence not triggering depreciation against which it is to be set."

SMA 4 was replaced in 1989 and 1990 by *Statements 4J, Accounting for Property, Plant, and Equipment, and 4L, Control of Property, Plant, and Equipment.* These two documents were prepared from a research project published by the IMA Research Committee, reporting control and analysis of property, plant, and equipment.

In other documents the discussion of accounting for fixed or physical assets is limited to a chapter or a few paragraphs in accounting texts. No lengthy document has been published that brings all the concepts of accounting for property, plant, and equipment together.

There are many articles on fixed assets in accounting magazines such as the *Management Accountant* published by the Institute of Management Accountants (IMA) and the *Journal of Accountancy*, published by the American Institute of Certified Public Accountants (AICPA). Most of these articles discuss theoretical issues of inflation accounting and depreciation.

There are a number of accounting courses offered by such organizations as the IMA, AICPA, and the American Management Association, as well as by a number of accounting and appraisal firms. However, these courses are mostly directed toward the tax requirements of accounting for depreciation. Similarly, there are numerous off-the-shelf personal computer programs aimed at fixed asset accounting. Again, the primary purpose is to fulfill tax requirements and generate depreciation entries. Only a few provide for comprehensive property records.

NEED TO CHANGE

It has become obvious that there is a need to change the manner in which management approaches long-term tangible assets. The many production facilities built in the United States are wearing out. Government infrastructures of roads, sewers, sidewalks, and utilities are all suffering from the concept of "put it in place and forget about it."

There is a need to get the most use out of these tangible assets. Much of the discussion having to do with inflation accounting for assets revolves around the problem that depreciation is not sufficient to cover the replacement costs of assets. The high cost of replacements, the dwindling supply of capital available, and high interest rates all require that new management control systems be put into place. With adequate control, management, and measurement of asset utilization, organizations can maximize the benefits from their investment in long-lived, tangible assets.

2

WHAT IS AN ASSET?

INTRODUCTION

According to the *Financial Accounting Standards Board Concepts Statement 6*, assets are "probable future economic benefits obtained or controlled by a particular entity as a result of past transactions or events." The *Institute of Management Accountants' Accounting Glossary* adds a second definition as "any owned physical object (tangible) or right (intangible) having economic value to its owners; an item or source of wealth with continuing benefits for future periods, expressed, for accounting purposes, in terms of its cost, or other value, such as current replacement cost. Future periods refers to the following year or years." SMA 2A

In its broadest sense, an asset is anything that will probably bring future economic benefit. In looking at assets, the focus will be on long-lived tangible assets, sometimes referred to as fixed assets or property, plant, and equipment.

Assets are classified into two categories: (1) tangible and (2) intangible. Tangible assets are assets that one can touch, hold, or feel. Typically called fixed assets in accounting literature, they are the physical things that a business uses in the production of goods and services. They constitute the production facilities, buildings, equipment, and vehicles. These operational assets of a business include furniture, computers, and similar items not used up within a year. Intangible assets are primarily financing items: stocks, bonds, mortgages, etc. These assets are outside the scope of this book.

Assets that are converted into cash during the normal production cycle are current. Current physical assets are referred to as financial

11

assets. These are physical assets such as raw materials, work in progress inventories, finished goods, and goods held for resale. Physical items can be financial assets, held in inventory, in one business, whereas in other businesses or applications they may be fixed assets. An example of such a financial asset would be real estate held in inventory by a real estate investment and sales organization or builder, which would be a fixed asset for everyone else. Equipment manufacturers have financial assets in finished goods or inventory held for sale, as well as plant and equipment that will be sold to other businesses. The inventory is a financial asset; when sold for use in a production line it becomes a fixed asset to the purchaser.

HISTORICAL COST

Historically, asset accounting has not stimulated the interest of accountants and managers in the United States. Assets have been analyzed in depth in terms of alternatives and appropriateness of the investment prior to purchase. However, once acquired and put in place, assets such as buildings, furniture, production equipment, and motor vehicles are not given much attention. Where management attention has been focused, it has been in terms of return on investment and major tax benefits, such as investment tax credits and accelerated depreciation expense allowed on tax returns. In fact, these government tax incentives to buy new equipment in order to stimulate the economy have influenced management to replace still-useful assets that have been depreciated on the tax records.

But there is a new perspective emerging on the part of managers and accountants with respect to fixed assets. The high initial cost to purchase, as well as the high carrying costs of debt, require a rethinking of the management of fixed assets. Many of the same factors that are bringing about just-in-time accounting philosophies and zero-defect quality control within the manufacturing process are also influencing managers' perspectives on asset management. Zero defects and quality circles of employees are aimed to reduce the high cost of less-than-perfect products and reflect today's need for greater precision. In order to accomplish this higher quality production, it is necessary to have high quality production equipment. This requires preventative maintenance to keep closer tolerances and less downtime. Equipment that fails during a production run leads to extremely high cost when the line stops. Preventative maintenance is being regularly scheduled on either an hours-of-use or calendar basis. This approach has begun to replace the attitude of put it in, use it, if it breaks repair it; if it breaks too many times, discard it and replace it.

In addition to the requirements of modern processing, a new perspective on the need to manage assets, those things that you have saved and paid for which will bring future benefits to the businesss, has come about as a result of the significant debt held by many businesses. The public's attention has been caught by the high government deficit, which must be financed by acquiring increasingly more debt. Large existing debt and the threat of higher interest rates on new debt due to the lower financial ratings are causing many managers to reconsider how to manage the assets they already have. Getting the maximum future value out of existing buildings and production equipment has become a more important aspect of management.

In addition to process requirements and debt concerns, the cost of disposal is also growing at an alarming rate. The United States produces 30 percent of the world's garbage, and its landfills are at capacity, forcing the creation of expensive new ones and making disposal of worn-out items more difficult. Replacing individual parts instead of entire machines will reduce the production of refuse.

In the past, accounting records of assets have been kept primarily for the purpose of establishing balance sheet amounts. The historical cost of purchasing or constructing the physical asset is included in the accounting property record. This amount, less depreciation, provides the basis for a return on investment calculation, the division of net assets (original cost less book depreciation) by net income.

The matching principle of accounting calls for the matching of costs with the accounting period those costs benefit. The purpose of the historical cost record is to ensure that the costs incurred in the purchase of assets in a past accounting period will be spread over the future accounting periods that benefit.

The costs recorded for each asset acquired include the purchase price and anything necessary to make it ready for production. All expenditures involved in the acquisition of an asset and getting it ready for use are capitalized as part of original cost. Included are the invoice price for the asset, transportation charges, and installation costs, including any construction or changes to the building necessary to house it. Other incidental costs are sales or use tax, duties on imported items, and testing and initial set-up costs. The total costs of acquiring and putting the asset into actual production use should be capitalized. The use in production at a reasonable production rate (as opposed to limited use during testing) is also the point where capitalization stops on the new asset and depreciation begins.

The cost of an asset must be spread on a rational, systematic basis over the periods of its useful life. This limited accounting application of historical cost records has led to many incorrect decisions regarding asset management. Recognizing this limitation, however, does not mean historical costs records are not necessary. Records must be established to provide information on location, maintenance history, and future usefulness of assets. Today's high costs of debt and the need to safeguard physical assets requires going beyond the matching principle in creating property records.

FIXED ASSETS

Historically, even the term accountants use for the long-lived tangible assets of business, that is, fixed assets, expressed the opinion that once purchased it is fixed, long term and does not require management attention. In the last few years, the more common "property, plant, and equipment" has been used to describe the operational assets of a business. Managers have found it necessary to provide additional information about property, plant, and equipment and created records separate from the accounting property record. Additional information includes current market value for insurance and security purposes, and utilization and maintenance records.

A single accounting record of tangible assets with normal accounting controls is far superior to multiple records. This integrated record with accounting controls has been made much simpler with the advent and widespread use of small computers. For example, recording maintenance expenses for large equipment items is now easy. In a motor vehicle fleet, actual maintenance costs can be recorded in the property record of each vehicle. This allows review to ensure preventative maintenance is scheduled and also to establish criteria for disposing of older motor vehicles when they are no longer economical to maintain. It then becomes possible to evaluate motor vehicles based on their entire maintenance record, rather than retiring vehicles based on age or mileage alone.

What are assets fixed in? Are they fixed in time, space, or value? It's really doubtful that they are fixed at all. IMA defines fixed assets as "noncurrent, nonmonetary tangible assets used in normal operations of a business." See property, plant, and equipment. SMA 2A.

Past practice has been to handle fixed assets as a "sunk cost." A past cost which cannot now be reversed and hence, should not enter into current decisions.

Differential cost is "the cost that is expected to be different if one course of action is adopted as compared with the costs of an alternative course of action; used in decision making. Contrast with sunk costs." SMA 2A.

If it is a fixed cost, then it's also a sunk cost. Is it really an asset if you can't sell it? If you can't move it, modify it, or maintain it? Those are alternative actions; therefore, historical cost of property, plant, and equipment are differential costs, not sunk costs. The term "fixed" cost implies a sunk cost.

This management treatment of fixed costs as sunk costs may encourage hostile takeovers using junk bonds. If the current management and stockholders ignore the alternative uses of their long-term tangible assets, an outsider may see a much greater short-term value. In a case like this the current managers and owners are treating the fixed assets as a sunk cost instead of a differential cost.

Few assets are fixed in any way. Most are mobile, and will disappear if not accounted for or deteriorate if not maintained. Many increase in value just because of inflation. If they don't increase in value, their replacement cost certainly increases. Typically, insurance policies require that coverage be at least 80 percent of replacement cost or recovery is limited to market value prior to the loss.

Even the government is learning that their fixed asset theory for infrastructure assets needs amendment. Roads, bridges, sewer plants, and buildings all seem to be in need of replacement at the same time.

15

This is occurring because they were put in place and ignored. No plan was prepared to manage them, to determine the best maintenance practice. Now they are not assets, but sources of liability. While government has a limited liability from suits due to personal injury resulting from improper maintenance of roads, etc., businesses do not enjoy this limitation. If an employee or customer is injured by one of your bridges, roads, or other holdings, you are responsible for the costs. Is that driveway or parking lot really a fixed asset? Or one to be managed so it will not become a liability?

It is difficult to imagine something that should be called a fixed asset. Assets are not fixed in any way, not in place, time, or future income or expense. The exception might be a work of art or historical treasure. However, even these items, if not protected, will deteriorate. In defining assets therefore, we shall use the terms property, plant, and equipment and avoid future use of the term "fixed" assets, which is in reality an obsolete term for property, plant, and equipment.

PROPERTY

Property includes lands and improvements thereon. Land is not depreciated and its cost lasts in our theoretical business model forever. The cost of land includes its acquisition cost, costs of appraising, recording, and obtaining title. It also includes the initial costs of making changes to it so that it can be used for the purpose intended. That includes the removal of old buildings, leveling, and perhaps the clean up of any toxic residue. When land is acquired together with buildings, the cost will be apportioned between the land and the buildings in proportion to their appraised value. If the acquisition plan contemplates the removal of the buildings, the total cost including removal is accounted for as cost of land. Any salvage value of the removed buildings, when disposed of, is deducted from the cost of the land.

Toxic residue cleanup provides a particular problem in accounting for land. If the extent of the toxic cleanup costs are known prior to purchase, it is assumed that the purchase price has been reduced accordingly. Then it is correct to include those cleanup costs in the cost of the land. However, where land is owned and toxic residues from past practice are discovered, the cleanup of these items provides no future value. Cleaning up these toxic wastes is similar to washing a rental car or limousine. You may not be able to generate any rental revenue without a clean and polished automobile, but it does not provide future value beyond that. Cleaning up toxic wastes makes the property usable, however it does not provide future benefit, it can only restore the usefulness of the property to its level of use prior to recognizing the toxic problem.

Improvements that theoretically have an indefinite life are also added to the cost of land. Grading, drainage, sewers, and utilities are examples. These items are put in once and unless damaged by force or disrupted by plans for new uses of the land, they do not require maintenance. Therefore, their life is assumed to be that of land forever in the accepted business model.

The proper treatment of property costs is an area that must be spelled out in the accounting manual for the firm so that all similar transactions are handled in the same way. The manual should translate these principles into specific accounting practices for the firm. For example, electric and gas utility installation to the meter or distribution point are usually a part of the land cost. Beyond this, location utilities and part of the individual building investment are to be included in the plant category.

The acquisition of property may bring about other expenditures which should be added to its historical cost. Some of these are:

Contract price

Real estate broker commissions

Legal fees involved in the transaction

Cost of title guaranty insurance policies

Cost of real estate surveys

Cost of an option that has been exercised

Special government assessments

Fees charged by government for changes in land use or zoning

Cost of removing buildings

Cost of cancellation of unexpired lease

Cost to move tenant if payable by purchaser

Payment of past due taxes if payable by purchaser

Cost of easements or rights of way

Assessments for the construction of public improvements

Deduction of salvage value from buildings removed and sold

Toxic waste cleanup

Grading land and providing drainage

Placing utilities

PLANT

The term "plant" has its origin in manufacturing, where the plant is literally used to house the production equipment. This includes buildings and other structures or improvements that have a limited life. Paved parking lots and sprinkler systems, as well as recreational and landscaping improvements, are included. Also included in plant are fences, roads, and grading and excavation costs necessary to construction of the buildings. The distinction between property (land) and plant is the duration of usefulness. Improvements to the property that will have a measurable or estimated life should be depreciated over that life. Therefore, they are charged to the plant account. If they are of indefinite life, they are treated as property.

All expenditures directly related to the purchase or construction of buildings or other physical plant are included in plant cost. Land includes the cost of preparation of a construction site. All costs for a specific construction are included in the cost of the product.

Some of the other expenditures that should be added to the capitalized cost of the asset acquired are:

Contract price or cost of construction

Cost of grading and excavation for the specific building

Expenses incurred in removing trees and other foliage for the specific building

Costs or remodeling on altering a purchased building to make it ready for use

Costs for architect's fees, plans, and other planning events

Cost of government fees and building permits

Payment of prior year taxes accrued on the building if payable by purchaser

Other costs such as security or temporary fencing, temporary buildings used during construction or other costs directly attributable to the construction or purchase of the specific building

Capitalized interest.

EQUIPMENT

Equipment includes the machinery, computers, office equipment, and all other long-lived items necessary for the operation of the business. These items require more managerial control because of their portability and general usefulness for other than the purpose intended when acquired. They range in price from a minimum capitalization level to many millions of dollars for complex production machinery. Because of the wide variety of requirements for different items of equipment we shall discuss them in several categories, including:

Tools

Building systems (heating, cooling, elevators)

Irrigation equipment

Furniture and office equipment

Computers

Printing presses

Automobiles

Tractors

Trucks

Trailers

Aircraft

Livestock

Furniture and Office Equipment

Furniture and office fixtures are long-lived assets needed to run a business. In the service industries, except for buildings, these will be the major tangible assets of the business. The establishment of a reasonable minimum capitalization level has to be weighed against the other factors of managing this class of equipment. Office desks and chairs that are personally used by one manager will receive the attention necessary to safeguard and ensure proper maintenance as required. Many companies establish a $5,000 minimum capitalization level for these items. However, telephone equipment purchased may become obsolete or require significant maintenance after some period of time. Also, office copiers, dictation machines, personal computers, and typewriters have a need for greater management and future planning. It is important that these items not all have a requirement for replacement in the same future year. Inclusion in the property record, which subjects such items to the controls provided in that system, may in fact reduce the dollar value at which it is desirable to maintain capitalization. These items should be included in a detailed policy and outlined in the handbook on asset capitalization or its chapter in the accounting policy manual of the business.

When the decision is made to capitalize a particular item of equipment, all of the costs involved in putting it into a condition ready for use should be included in the asset value.

Some of the costs that may be incurred are:

Contract price

Commissions paid

Legal fees and other contract costs

Cost of title guaranty insurance policies

Cost of transferring title

Freight, handling, and storage costs

Sales or use tax and other taxes or fees assessed

Costs of preparation of the space for installation (foundations, special walls, removal of windows)

Use of cranes or other means of putting in place

Installation charges

Cost of testing and preparation for use

Costs of reconditioning used equipment purchased

DEFINING ASSETS

Assets are not always easily defined. For example, a Berkeley, California producer of "baby" vegetables for New York City upscale restaurants could not function without the regular dependable inexpensive air shuttle of the crop each morning. The New York restaurants pay a premium for the product, but it must be picked that morning and delivered to New York City by noon for serving in restaurants that evening. Is the transportation link from San Francisco airport to New York an asset of this Berkeley producer? From an accounting sense, it is not. However, it continues to deliver future benefits to the company. Without that transportation link being available there would be no business, but it would be impossible to establish any value to that transportation link without a sale.

If the business were to be sold, it is likely to command as an operating business more than the value of its individual components. This additional value will be included on the purchaser's balance sheet as goodwill. Much of that goodwill can be a result of an existing working transportation system from the producer's garden to the upscale restaurants.

Goodwill is an intangible asset. Accounting recognizes it only because there has been an actual payment for it. It must be recognized somehow as its usefulness is used up over future periods. The asset exists whether it is recognized in the book of accounts as goodwill or not. However, this emphasizes the accounting concept of recognizing asset *value* in accounting systems for the purpose of measuring the decrease in its future usefulness in relationship to its original cost. In this case, it is not a problem in defining the asset, but in establishing the asset's value.

There are other difficulties in defining an asset. In industries where investment in property, plant, and equipment is low in comparison to return on products, there has been no need to closely manage the investment in assets. Examples are restaurants where investment is limited to leasehold improvements. The concern of restaurant managers is keeping their lease and labor costs down. The investment in fixed assets required to run a substantial restaurant is small in comparison to its gross sales.

The investment in leasehold improvements for a restaurant many times are sunk costs. They have value only to the end of the lease. It may also be desirable for marketing purposes to substantially alter them prior to the end of their useful life. Here the value is easily established based on what they cost to install. However, they might not be providing future benefits and therefore require replacement before their costs have been recognized.

A different management problem exists where investment in capital items is large relative to the cost of production or where there are few other opportunities to use the assets for different purposes. Examples are oil refineries and pharmaceutical laboratories. Once the refinery or drug production facilities are constructed, they are not readily usable for any other purpose. There is also little opportunity to make decisions relative to alternative use of these assets. A grocery store location could be altered to become a restaurant or a hardware store. However, an oil refinery could cost more to dismantle than it originally cost to construct.

These cases raise the question of the value of alternative uses. The accounting principle of recognizing decline in service value through depreciation takes this into account in the concept of salvage value. Salvage value is the value which the asset has at the end of its useful life. The oil refinery would have a negative salvage value and current discussion is aiming at requiring recognition of the cost of its dismantling and toxic cleanup in depreciation expense.

This entire area has been clouded by the tax considerations. The Internal Revenue Service (IRS) will not allow the recognition for tax purposes. However, that is not justification for failing to recognize this negative salvage value in the accounting process and definition of assets. However, this is not really a definition of asset problem, it is evidence to support investigation into the recognition of the liability as it is being created. Problems of contamination be it by petroleum products, or nuclear waste must be included in the discussion and recognized in accounting for liabilities, not in the establishment of an assets definition or value.

GOVERNMENT ACCOUNTING

The Government Accounting Standards Board (GASB) specifies the generally accepted accounting principles applicable to government accounting. The Board has created a separate category of infrastructure fixed assets which are "immovable and of value only to the government unit." It has authorized the non-reporting of these items in government financial statements for units other than enterprise funds. (Enterprise funds are universities, sewage disposal, airports, and other entities similar to businesses.) The logic is that items such as sidewalks, roads, etc. are a value only to the government unit and cannot be readily sold or converted into cash and would not be subject to easy loss or destruction. These types of assets, if recorded, are kept in a general fixed asset account group (GFAAG). This is an auxiliary record that may be maintained at historical costs. It is not required. Many governments are choosing to keep adequate records of all assets although they are allowed not to report such assets. Failure to keep a property record of assets may lead to poor management of these assets. Loss of asset value and use result from inadequate maintenance and general neglect. Therefore, the current trend in government accounting as well as nonprofit accounting is to adopt good property records practices similar to those developed for business. Although a growing number of government and nonprofit managers are choosing to adopt the same practices and principles as outlined throughout this book, most follow governmental accounting guidelines outlined by the Government Finance Officer's Association. They expense all capital purchases in the current period and maintain a side record. No depreciation is recognized on these investments in property, plant, and equipment.

Government accounting practice has been to buy an asset, charge it to the current period, and use it up. No thought to managing that asset, nor depreciating it over its future useful periods was given. A lack of management of these assets is now bringing them all to maturity at the same time. This has produced an infrastructure that has been inadequately maintained and, of necessity, must continue long beyond its useful life because no thought or planning has been given for replacements.

For a business, an asset is an item that will provide future benefits. It has an estimated life beyond one year and some minimum value. This definition also holds true in government and nonprofit accounting. In government accounting, however, assets are not capitalized and depreciated in the accounting records except in enterprise funds. They are charged in full against the general fund as an expense when acquired. These assets are then listed in the general fixed assets account group at original cost, or fair market value at time of donation, to the government entity. No depreciation is charged on assets or in the general fixed asset account group. The general fund is not affected by assets except in the period acquired.

USER FEES

A change in philosophy is developing that all government services should not be paid for on the basis of generalized taxes paid by all citizens. Instead user fees should provide for many of the specific services. In order to deliver an adequate basis for establishing fees that cover the cost of services, governments must be able to determine the value of the assets used in the period in which the fee is to be assessed. Examples of such fees are building inspection, charges for coping government reports, and special roadwork repair to accommodate a specific project. Cost-based pricing systems need to recognize depreciation of government-owned assets. Such considerations are leading government managers to change past practices.

NOT-FOR-PROFIT ACCOUNTING

Many nonprofit organizations do not require formal audited financial statements. As a result, informal, less-than-adequate bookkeeping systems are used. Those that receive funds from the U.S. government, including most private schools, hospitals, rest homes, and many social services organizations, are required to have audited statements.

Many nonprofit organizations receive grants and other donations of assets. These donated assets must be placed on the books at current market price or recognized at a reasonable value. Techniques for establishing this value are outlined in Chapter 7, "Establishing Asset Value." There should be no differences in accounting for and managing assets in a nonprofit organization and a business. The same generally accepted accounting principles apply.

From a practical point of view, this causes some problems. Let's look at an example of a small farmer's marketing association. The association promotes the on-farm sales of their members by printing and distributing a map of the county with the location and description of each farm. The association holds a farm fair each year to generate the funds to run the organization and membership dues provide the rest of the income.

The assets of the association are the map and its trademarked name, cash, supplies, and equipment used to operate the fair. Food stands, the electrical distribution system, and signs, are all examples of the association's assets. For personal property tax purposes the assets are valued at $16,500. However, no value is carried on the books. As with governmental fund accounting, these items were expensed as purchased. Others were constructed by members with donated labor and material. Is there any benefit to the board of directors to have a property record of these items? Is there a need to show the depreciation expense in subsequent years' reports?

Establishing controls to ensure that these assets do not disappear is important. The association does not have a dedicated office or place of business where these assets are stored. Unless a property record is maintained, the best memory of members is all they have. The fair equipment is only used once a year and is stored at a member's farm the rest of the time. It can easily be lost if the storing member moves or transfers it to another member without record. The part-time staff do not have equipment storage and maintenance as a specific duty. The fair manager, of course, has an interest in knowing where these assets are, the state of repair, and future usefulness.

The elected board of directors must know the future life expectancy to plan for the equipment's replacement.

There is a need then to define physical assets in these nonprofit organizations as they would be defined in a business.

3

CLASSIFICATIONS OF ASSET TRANSACTIONS

INTRODUCTION

When a business event occurs that affects the physical assets of the company, it must be recorded in the books of account. This is done by classifying and coding the transaction.

Classification of a transaction is defined as

> The identification of each item and the systematic placement of like items together according to their common feature. Items grouped together under common heads are further defined according to their fundamental differences. *IMA CLASSIFICATIONS AND CODING FOR ACCOUNTING OPERATIONS*, page 5

The classification process identifies transactions so that they may be assigned to individual codes, stored in accounting databases, and retrieved at a later date. The coding systems allow identification and manipulation of raw accounting data in a fashion that allows management to base decisions on the data.

A standardized identification system of assets must be established. This will provide a means to identify, select, and assign the numerous accounting codes to transactions. The purchase, transfer, or disposition of an item of property, plant, or equipment must be recorded by the accounting system.

The classification system must be designed to produce consistent coding of similar transactions. The system must allow different people over wide time frames to arrive at the same classification for similar transactions.

It is necessary to make it easy for the person handling the transaction to classify and identify the correct code. Their main concern is to use the asset, not classify and code it. Because these functions are generally not done by accountants, there is a need for good guidance in the accounting manuals. Special emphasis should be placed on the creation of the coding and classification systems.

It is important to note that if an expense item is incorrectly classified, it only affects one accounting period. However, misclassification of an asset fails to enter it in the proper property record and therefore does not establish the controls of that asset. The lack of management and control mechanisms may mean that the asset is not put to its best use. It also may trigger incorrect personal or property taxes on the business. Likewise, faulty coding means that depreciation expense and other performance measurements of the business will be incorrect.

The identification of a base unit is particularly important on purchase and disposition transaction.

The classification process will establish the characteristics of business events that must be accounted for. Property, plant, and equipment are the largest classes of physical assets. Each of these classes must be broken down into logical parts. Property includes land, grading, pavement, drainage, for example; equipment is a very broad class. Subgroups must be established based on the type of business and the needed reports.

CLASSIFICATION SYSTEMS

Classification systems must define to the lowest level that which will be required for aggregation analysis of the data after it has been placed in the property record. Because most assets will also be recorded in a property record system, a number of identification codes must be assigned. The classification must include the general ledger account, property type, its use, location, activity, and department. It will be necessary to review required reports for GAAP, tax authorities, property control, depreciation studies, etc. Review of the many report requirements will establish the lowest level of detail that must be separately identified and coded.

28

In designing a classification system for property, plant, and equipment, it is not possible to divorce it from the remainder of the accounting system. The general ledger accounts typically are the major classifications. Within each of those classifications, it will be necessary to identify those things that are unique to the particular business. Although this discussion is confined to classifications for property, plant, and equipment, an overall accounting classifications process must be in place in the company. The overall accounting classifications process should be established and documented at least at the general ledger account level prior to attempting to create one specifically for property, plant, and equipment.

The classification system should be designed by accountants but requires the assistance of operating management. The people most knowledgeable about how to identify items must be involved in the process. An accountant need not know in detail how the theory of electronics or quantum physics works to classify exotic things. However, someone who understands the minutiae of the business must assist in designing a classification system for a company that utilizes significant numbers of exotic items.

The classification system must be documented in the accounting or property record manual.

In establishing the classification system, distinctions must be made between characteristics of physical items. Examples are mobile versus fixed equipment. In motor vehicles, licensed versus those not requiring licenses. In the manufacturing process, production equipment should be in a different classification from research or laboratory equipment. Some businesses will require distinguishing between different types of property. In one business, a characteristic may be important enough to be separately distinguished. In other businesses, that characteristic will have little or no importance.

The best way to understand why two different types of businesses have different classification needs, is to look at an example. In a transportation firm, it will be important for the classification of motor vehicles to distinguish between those used to carry passengers versus ones used for freight. A car rental firm will have automobiles classified as rental. Identical automobiles may also be in their property record as used for administrative purposes. The classification system should provide two separate classes for automobiles. Rental cars and administrative-use cars. This is an example of a sub-classification by use.

A transportation firm involved in carrying freight will probably require a distinction between light versus heavy trucks. It is likely that the useful life of heavy trucks will be greater than those of light trucks. When life, use, and depreciation method must be differentiated, then these characteristics must be separately identified within the classification system.

For example:

Motor vehicles
    Carrier vehicles
        Passenger vehicles
            Vans
            Buses
            Taxis
        Freight
            Heavy truck
            Light truck

Businesses not in the transportation industry will have different characteristics that will need to be identified in vehicles. A typical classification scheme may be:

Motor vehicles
    Autos and trucks
    Shop vehicles

Because vehicles are not of major importance in the non-transportation business, it is not necessary to distinguish between as many characteristics.

Review of your specific business' needs in terms of characteristics to be identified is important. Some assistance may be available to you in industry publications. A number of recommended classification systems have been established for particular industries. Suggested charts of accounts for your type of organization in AISCP

Industry Accounting manuals or in manuals published by professional organizations, such as the Government Finance Officers Association, or those in the Code of Federal Regulation for Regulated Utilities may be a good starting point for looking at your classification design. However, just like the charts of accounts that are in off-the-shelf computer systems, they should be viewed as a starting point. None of them will contain all of the distinctions and separation of characteristics needed by your particular company.

ACCOUNTING POLICY DECISIONS

Each organization will have different needs. You must review your company's accounting policies. If they are not already in place, they should be established and documented. In establishing a classification system for physical assets, the capitalization policy is of prime importance. It will be of significance whether the classification distinction between capitalized assets and expensed assets is $100 or $5,000. The procedures for establishing the capitalization policy are covered in Chapter 4 of this book. We will not discuss them here. However, it is important to note that a policy must be definitive, written, and documented. It will establish the parameters for classification. If all items over $100 are to be capitalized, then it is not likely that any expense items will be contained in the property record. However, if a capitalization policy for your organization requires expensing of all individual items less than $5,000, then it is likely that your property record will contain items that have been expensed. These different situations establish different classification characteristics that must be identified as well as a different design for your property record.

In order to assign a unique code to a transaction characteristic, it must be identified in the classification and coding system. Output reports can provide groupings in any combination that are separately classified and coded. Unless a separate classification is identified and a code assigned, there can be no separate identification on a report. Any item that is coded individually can be separately identified or aggregated and shown in total by some grouping.

State and local tax laws will establish characteristics that must be identified in the classification system. In order to establish within the property record system a control mechanism that street-operated motor vehicles are properly licensed, that characteristic must be separately identified. Similarly, real estate and personal property tax are applied by many jurisdictions to business property. Where a different tax rate or reporting on tax reports is required, that characteristic must be included.

The depreciation methods used for different types of physical assets must also be considered. Each type of property that utilizes a different depreciation method should be separately identified. Similarly, items with different useful lives should have a means within the classification system of separate identification of that characteristic.

Each general ledger and subgroup within the accounting system must be separately identified. The account code itself is typically the largest classification grouping. However, in some organizations, the account code is used for all distinctions of characteristics. That makes for a lengthy account code and complexity in its assignment. Most organizations, as outlined in other chapters, will find it more appropriate to have separate codes with separate fields individually assigned to identify the many characteristics.

Capital Budget Categories

It will be necessary to review the organization's capital budget requirements and identify those characteristics that must be separately identified. In order to make capital budget decisions, it is necessary to aggregate and review past expenditures. Similarly, the maintenance expense on different physical items will be important in projecting what future capital expenditures must be budgeted for. In most organizations, the capital budget will not identify additional items for classifications. The capital budgeting process is typically done in a more aggregated fashion. However, an organization that does research in other than a dedicated organization may require a separate budget report identification on research equipment. In other organizations, the department responsible for research is identified and the budget created by that organization. Some means must therefore be available to separately classify by organization as a budget category.

Items of physical property subjected to different inventory controls should also be identified with separate classes. Some property will require a specific physical inventory to establish its location and existence. Other items such as furniture in large meeting rooms or cafeterias may only be maintained in aggregate without annual verification requirements. In establishing the classification system, review the different inventory methods used and establish a classification for each method.

Property security and internal control procedures should be reviewed. Items of high value and portability may require not only greater inventory controls, but also security. Computers and other small electronic devices require greater control procedures. Businesses operating in remote areas such as construction, mining, and timber companies may require different security and control procedures for equipment left in those locations. Airlines and aircraft rental companies managing fleets of aircraft have special internal control, security, and inventory problems with component electronic devices in the aircraft. They are typically removed and replaced for maintenance, have easy portability, are high cost, and can be transferred to other uses and therefore should be separately controlled. These needs must be considered in establishing classification system design. Government organizations involved in law enforcement as well as private security companies should consider their control procedures for safety equipment. Items like firearms will have special classification requirements.

Having identified these characteristics within the classification system allows transactions to be separately coded, stored in accounting databases, and retrieved at a later date. The purpose of classification has been to group, compare, and display the data. The result will be the creation of reports to assist in analysis and decision making.

CODING OF TRANSACTIONS

The classification system should be documented in the accounting or property record manual. It can then be used as the basis for the definitions of items that will be individually coded. The various codes are the means of shorthand communication with the accounting system, be it manual or on computer. Each classification category and subgrouping must be documented. Included should be a definition and brief description of each item.

Accountants design and provide the classification and coding systems with the assistance of others. The coding is primarily accomplished by nonaccountants. Purchasing agents and others that purchase, modify, repair, move, and dispose of the company's physical assets will generally do the coding of those transactions.

In establishing definitions and coding systems, it is important to keep in mind that the person handling the transaction must be able to simply identify the correct code and assign it to the transaction.

Coding of accounting transactions is defined as "the assignment of numbers, letters, or other symbols according to a systematic plan for distinguishing the classifications to which each item belongs and for distinguishing items within a given classification from each other." (Page 6, *IMA Classification and Coding for Accounting Operations*)

The coding should be placed on the document that authorizes purchase or transfer of the item. The purchase of new equipment may be coded on either the ordering document, or an invoice which will be processed for payment. In addition to handling payment or creating an accounts payable record, the new asset record should be established within the property record.

Provide information for the person coding the documents on who to consult on unusual transactions. On unusual or unique transactions, such as purchase or construction of land or buildings, it may be necessary for the asset accountant to be contacted for his or her opinion on the correct coding. However, for most transactions, the definitions documented in the assets accounting manual should make it simple to identify the appropriate codes and place them on the correct accounting document. Remember, the aggregate of the mini transactions that are being coded provide the information on which decisions are based. The accounting results and measurement of the organization will be significantly affected by the quality of the coding decisions.

The distinguishing attributes that are of significance to the user or purchaser of the item should be easily established. The various coding systems must then be documented in a fashion that allows easy access to a definition that is meaningful to the person doing the coding.

PROPERTY RECORD CODING SYSTEM

The individual characteristics that have been identified in designing the classification system must be represented in the coding scheme. The following are examples of transaction code; your organization's system may well have additional unique requirements.

Property record class
> Land, building, furniture, motor vehicle, construction equipment, etc.

Asset identification number (tag number)
> Unique number sequentially assigned to each property record item

Property type
> Taxes—real, personal, lease, etc.

Location code
> Address, building, floor, tax district

Organization code
> Code to identify the organization responsible, typically hierarchical code

Custodian identification
> Code to identify department custodian (may be last name)

Description code
> Acquit to standard descriptions included in the asset manual

Date of acquisition
> Invoice or delivery date

Historical (book) cost
> Cost to put in service per GAAP

Name of vendor or manufacturer

Estimated salvage value

Proceeds expected from sale at end of useful life

Estimated economic life

Expected length of life in years

Depreciation method
FIT, state, book, straight line, accelerated, etc.

Costs of reproduction new and date established
Appraised value on date, used to determine cost to replace

Insurance coverage
Value for insurance, cost of reproduction less self-insured increment

Maintenance expense record by year
Expenditures on maintenance from original placement or last X years

Estimated deferred maintenance
Annual assessment to return to top condition

Leased property
Indicator of leased property to be controlled, but not depreciated

Expensed item
Not depreciated, but controlled

Examples of coding systems that might be used follow:

SAMPLE GENERAL LEDGER CHART OF ACCOUNTS

11000	Property
11100	Land
11110	Grading
11120	Drainage
11130	Removal of buildings
11140	Toxic cleanup
11150	Preparation for intended use
11199	Other
11200	Improvement to land
11210	Landscaping
11220	Grading
11230	Retaining walls

11240	Roads, parking lots & sidewalks
11250	Utilities
11260	Culverts, catch basins, trenches
11270	Railroad sidings
11290	Other
12000	Plant
12100	Buildings and other structures
12110	Leasehold improvements
12120	Air conditioning & heating units
12130	Attached, integral part
12131	Wiring
12132	Electrical lighting systems
12133	Boilers
12134	Plumbing
12135	Fire protection systems
12140	Passenger Elevators
13000	Equipment
13100	Mobile
13110	Forklifts
13120	Tractors
13130	Electronic test equipment
13140	Garage equipment
13200	Machinery
	Tools
	Power saws
	Planers
	Welders
	Tooling
13300	Computers
13400	Aircraft
	Electronics
	Radios
	Survival equipment
	Engines
13500	Furniture
	Office
	Fine arts
	Rugs

	Tables
	Computer desks
	Chairs
13600	Fixtures
	Drapes
	Lighting systems
13700	Production equipment
13800	Vehicles
13810	Large trucks
13820	Autos
13830	Light trucks

4

DETERMINING BASE UNIT

INTRODUCTION

In establishing a consistent asset policy, the determination of base units is of prime importance. The base unit is the smallest asset component. It is the basic unit in which the property records are maintained.

The definition and policies for establishing base units should be written by the asset manager and accountant. It should be reviewed and approved by the company's senior management. The policies that establish the base unit will have a long-term impact on the decision of what to capitalize versus expense in the current period. This will have great impact on the company's financial results. It also affects the ability to control assets and the expense of the asset accounting process. The base unit is the smallest item capitalized. All components of a base unit are capitalized as part of the base unit in initial purchase. Subsequent replacements of components will be expensed when purchased.

DEFINITION OF BASE UNIT

Little authoritative documentation has been done on establishing a base unit. The only definition currently cited is contained in the Institute of Management Accountants (IMA) "Statement on Management Accounting 4J." It states "Base unit . . . is the least expensive cost objective to be capitalized. If a computer system is capitalized as a single asset, then the computer system is a base unit. If a central processor (CPU), the disk drives, and each work station are recorded as separate assets, then a CPU is a base unit as are the disk drives and work stations."

The definition of cost objective is "a function, organizational subdivision, contract, product or other work unit for which arrangement is made to accumulate and measure cost. (*IMA Statement on Management Accounting 2*)

These definitions provide evidence of the difficulty in documenting the concept of base unit. *Webster's New World Dictionary* has the word defined as "1 to determine or set down the boundaries of: set down or show the precise outlines of. 2 to determine and state the limits and nature of; describe exactly. 3 to give the distinguishing characteristics of."

It is easy to apply these definitions for a specific base unit. A computer or a disk drive can be described exactly. Its limits are precisely established. However, it is quite another thing to write a definition of the generalities of a base unit. A base unit can be an entire building or each of its components, an entire assembly line or its components.

The definition of a base unit must be established for each individual company. In this chapter, the elements that must be considered and how a general definition may be written will be discussed. However, each industry and each company within it will have different requirements.

PURPOSE OF A BASE UNIT

Base unit definition is the necessary element of a consistent capitalization policy. Once a base unit is established it should not be changed, unless there is a significant reason.

In establishing the formal policy, two main factors should be considered:

1. Record-keeping costs—very small base units will necessitate large numbers of assets records. This will increase the cost of maintaining that accounting system.

2. Value of the detailed information—value can be measured in many different ways. The value of an asset can be the replacement cost. It can also be the cost if the equipment breaks down because preventative maintenance was not performed or if legally required maintenance must be accomplished at a time when the asset is needed on line. An example of this would be an aircraft that must have maintenance checks each 100 hours. It is important to schedule this when the craft is not needed for a scheduled flight. Another cost is having an item in the right place when required. Construction equipment such as cranes or graders have a large carrying cost. If the one needed on a construction job in one city or state is at another location, considerable expense can be incurred while a crew waits for it to be delivered. All of these costs should be considered in determining not only the information to be maintained in the property record, but also establishment of a base unit. The base unit definition will determine what items are given individual property record identification and control. In the case of an aircraft, engines also have required major maintenance intervals. Normally, spare engines are maintained. At the appropriate maintenance interval, engines are swapped, the aircraft continues on with a new engine while the one removed is overhauled. It is important in this case to actually maintain the engine as the base unit and control it as an individual item.

The ability to control an asset, in many cases, provides much more benefit than the cost of maintaining an additional record. However, the cost of control is not just the computer record. The major cost is in ensuring that the record is maintained. The location of a major piece of construction equipment must be reported each time it is moved, if information on its whereabouts is to be available. The cost of making such a report, and following up to ensure the report is made, could be of greater cost than the value of the information produced. If a company owns only one or two cranes and they have a single operator, other means of ensuring that equipment is in the right location are possible. The operator can be given the schedule of when and where the equipment should be available. However, for a company that has a number of pieces that must be juggled between jobs, not by the operator, but by project managers, the cost of keeping the file updated will be negligible in comparison to not having equipment at a location when it is needed.

Maintaining adequate asset records for tax purposes is necessary. Tax depreciation may be different from that required for accounting books. Sufficient detail should be maintained so that the tax return can be prepared from the information in the property record. In establishing a base unit, consideration of tax rules are important.

A building might be established as a single base unit with its furnishings separately identified. However, tax depreciation will be different for the building itself than for heating and air conditioning units, as well as lighting, refrigeration, and other built-in systems. The tax rules are established to accomplish government policies not based on any accounting logic. Periodically, the government establishes investment tax credits to encourage businesses to purchase assets. These credits allow profitable companies to reduce the cost of their assets through a reduction in taxes. Typically, the rules apply to assets with lives greater than five years. Consideration of making individual items that have in the past or may in the future be eligible for investment tax credits is an appropriate exercise in establishing a base unit.

Underlying accounting principles also will affect the definition of base units.

Materiality

We should not spend money to keep records that would not alter decisions. In the past, assets have not received much management attention. They are receiving more attention today because of the high cost of debt. The past practice of ignoring assets is now material. Many companies, in addition to government entities, have taken the attitude in the past of purchasing assets, installing them, and ignoring them. Now, companies need to make up for deferred maintenance. The replacement of assets all at the same time is becoming a material concern.

The reduction in cost of maintaining records due to the introduction of personal computers is significant. Asset software is now catching up with the technical computer improvements and there are accounting systems that can be purchased relatively inexpensively for integrated asset modules within complete accounting systems. Similarly, the reduction of cost of maintaining those records through "one write" systems that capture changes in assets through routine accounting entries has reduced record-keeping costs. Asset databases are now updated from purchase and maintenance documents that are required for other than asset record-keeping purposes.

Consistency

Reports must be produced on a comparable basis. In order or accomplish this, transactions of a similar nature must be handled in the same way even by different people and in different time periods. For this to happen, written policies must be produced and must be taken into consideration in defining base units. The designation of a base unit and its property record class must be easily discernable by different people. What is easily discernable by an asset manager or accountant, may not be understood by purchasing agents, mechanics, and managers.

Full Disclosure

The information presented in reports must include everything an informed reader needs to arrive at a conclusion. Nothing of substance should be concealed or omitted. Establishment of base units has an impact on the material that can be produced. Leverage buyouts that have had such an impact on our economy during the 1980s were, in many cases, made possible by the lack of disclosure regarding assets. Financial statements only contained the depreciated historical cost. Present management had no idea of their current market value. Establishment of very large base units in terms of dollars can perpetuate the lack of disclosure. This principle is also cited as a reason that historical cost is not an adequate measure of the value of assets. In determining what is a base unit, consideration should be given to separating items that will have material future value versus those that do not. An example might be a light utility pickup. The future value of the pickup will be based on the depreciated value in the used marketplace. However, a utility bed, generator, or hydraulic crane attached to the pickup may have a considerably different value based on future utility. Separate base units should be established based on the expected life of an item in addition to its expected value at the end of that period. Another example is in furniture: hardwood furniture not subject to damage may have greater market value in twenty years than it had at the time of purchase. A service organization, such as a real estate firm, may have a significantly higher market value in fully depreciated office furniture. Furniture in a department store or an office environment where it is subject to considerable wear and tear will not have much future value. In many businesses, furniture will be an item to lump together, with little reason for spending the cost of maintaining individual property records.

Full disclosure is appropriate when viewing financial statements as a whole. Statements that contain so much detail as to be overwhelming to the reader are of no use. They also increase costs beyond any benefit. This is a significant reason for not capitalizing each small item used for a period longer than one year.

Objective

A written set of decision rules for classification of each transaction is necessary. The person making the classification decision must be able to follow these rules and arrive at the same conclusions regarding similar assets in different time periods. These rules must also allow different people to arrive at the same conclusion.

ESTABLISHING BASE UNITS

In establishing the list of base units for your organization make decisions using specific criteria.

The estimated life of a base unit and its components should be the same. All components of a base unit should have the same depreciation life. Tax and accounting depreciation will be different for the same base unit. However, all components of a base unit should have the same tax life. It should also have only one accounting depreciation life, even though different from tax life.

A base unit must be readily identifiable. It must be distinguishable from other similar items and it must be readily apparent to the observer. In the personal computer example, a simple processing unit, disk drive, and monitor all contained in the same computer box are not readily identifiable. They appear to be all one item to the casual observer because disassembly would be necessary to make separate units. Even more difficult is the installed computer card to provide additional capability. Examples are telephone modems, additional storage, or automatic processing functions. The base unit must be subject to verification of its existence without disassembly.

Aircraft, manufacturing production lines, and complex equipment may pose difficulty in meeting this criteria. In contrast to the personal computer, is an aircraft with four or six engines. Engines are readily identifiable and can have separate serial numbers; individual radio equipment within an aircraft may be more difficult to establish. Telephone switching systems may all be located within a single cabinet much like a personal computer. Capabilities of handling ten, twenty, or one hundred telephones may be added to the cabinet without any external modification. If these items have material value and a need for control, they should be individually identified. Establishing separate base units may also require education of the people responsible for those assets in order that their existence can be verified periodically.

Minimum Capitalization Policy

The value of a base unit should generally be no less than the minimum capitalization policy established. Typically this minimum would be between $1,000 and $5,000. Any amount less than the minimum capitalization policy should be expensed. However, in establishing base units for your company, this minimum would not be rigidly adhered to. A $5,000 part of the airframe of a $5,000,000 aircraft is not material. If one part must be present for the aircraft to be operational and it is not subject to further need for control, there is no reason to consider less than the entire airframe one base unit. However, a $3,000 radio set, life raft, and other emergency equipment contained in the aircraft may be an appropriate separate base unit. Factors other than a reasonable minimum capitalization level are ability to control, the possibility of getting lost, etc.

Similarly, maintenance requirements and the ability to check that necessary maintenance is accomplished must be taken into consideration. Individual components of a manufacturing production line will have differing maintenance requirements. Personal computers, disk drives, molding, and welding or fabrication equipment may have little maintenance need. However, the components that do the fabrication may have close tolerances that should be ensured on a specific interval of calendar time, hours of use, or a combination thereof. Components that have different maintenance requirements should be established as distinct base units.

For some items, there are legally required maintenance intervals. In addition to aircraft, large trucks operating on the highway must have periodic maintenance as well as inspections to ensure they are within tolerance. These inspections may be performed by state inspection stations on a calendar basis; they may also be performed by employees certified as mechanics or inspectors. Records must be maintained and must be available when requested. Individual components such as tractors, trailers, airframes, engines, and electronic equipment with legally required maintenance or inspections should be established as separate base units.

Industry practices must also be taken into consideration. In the cattle industry, different practices exist for the commercial breeder who produces meat to eat versus the registered breeder who produces genetic improvements in breeding cattle. The commercial breeder typically maintains records of a cow and calf unit until the calf is weaned and then will keep a record of the year's production of steer calves. The registered breeder, however, will create a new asset record for each calf as it is born. The difference in the industry is the relative value of a new calf, which will vary from $200 or $300 for a commercial breeder to $15,000 or $100,000 for the registered breeder. Also, individual records of the lineage of the new registered calf are necessary. The recording of individual birth dates, weaning weight, and birth weights contributes to the value of the registered breeding animal.

Similarly, aircraft and trucks have periodic maintenance routines that may keep them in usefulness well beyond their depreciation life. Practice in the industry requiring legal inspections and continuous maintenance will keep these assets in use well beyond reasonable depreciation lives.

In some government units, it is necessary to maintain base units of small and inexpensive items. Examples are police and fire safety equipment. Pistols and revolvers, oxygen units, and other small items must be controlled for security reasons.

Nonprofit organizations may find it necessary to have base units that are much smaller than their capitalization minimum. For example, a nonprofit trade or marketing association that maintains assets necessary to put on periodic fairs or educational activities may have many items whose original cost is less than $100. The fact that these items are stored in members' donated buildings requires greater control efforts. One nonprofit organization that conducts a fair annually to raise the funds for its promotion and advertising events has such a system. The assets consist of portable fencing and booths with walls, windows, and roofs to meet food handling requirements. They also have installed lighting and underground electrical wires in the local park where the fair is held. The portable lighting booths and fencing are stored in one or more members' barns throughout the year. As the needs of the members change, these items may be moved. The institutional memory is dependent upon volunteer managers that change from year to year, or a detailed asset record. Most of these assets were expensed as they were created. Lumber and wire were purchased typically in less than $200 or $300 increments and the booths were then constructed. However, in order to know the location of the asset and its condition, the organization found it necessary to create an asset record. Many of these items have been carried at a historical cost of zero indicating their original expense. There is also a requirement in this jurisdiction for businesses as well as nonprofit organizations to maintain records of personal property and pay a tax to the county. A property record substantiates the existence of the items, but a zero-value entry in the property record substantiates not paying personal property tax.

Each individual booth, however, is maintained as a property record item (base unit), and condition, estimated need for replacement, etc. is maintained in the property record for each item.

DECISION RULES

A prime consideration in documenting the rules for determining base units and the list of base units by property class is that they are understandable by the nonaccountants in purchasing management and production. The means of identification should also be useful to those who are using the assets. Examples are individual works of art that are numbered and identified versus a flock of breeding hens, which may have leg bands designating the particular hatch they came from.

Each base unit must be identifiable by some means on invoices that document its purchase, move, and retirement. Some means of identification is necessary to distinguish each individual base unit from similar ones.

Controllability depends on the environment in which the asset is used. Fish in the ocean or birds loose in the wild are not controllable. It is no different from small tools used by construction crews that move from place to place and are used by many employees.

In some cases, the environment can be established to improve the controllability and reduce the number of base units required. For example, in high school vocational classes, it has long been the practice to have tool cribs. One person passes out the tools at the beginning of each period and is responsible for ensuring that they are back in the crib hanging in a specific spot at the end of the period. Typically, these shops have a designated spot for each tool with its outline drawn, and if one is missing it is immediately obvious. A different approach is used by libraries, where an individual record of the book and its whereabouts is maintained. In the case of the tool crib, the review procedure eliminates the need for an individual record of the asset because it can be controlled by its environment. However, in the library situation, a record must be maintained in order to know whether the book is in its place on the library shelf.

DIFFICULTIES IN ESTABLISHMENT

Establishing the exact level of detail that is appropriate for a particular business is difficult. It will also vary by asset categories. For some categories it would be particularly difficult to find a record-keeping basis that is meaningful to the individuals using them. A maintenance document prepared to record an employee's time is self-policing. If a document is not filed the employee will not be paid.

There is no reason not to include the asset that had maintenance performed on it on the employee's record. Also, where repair parts must be requisitioned, that document can contain the identification of the assets worked on. However, when neither of these conditions exist, it may be necessary to have a document prepared that is only processed by the asset property record. Movement of assets from one location to another may not be connected with any other transaction. Creating documents just to maintain property record information will substantially increase the cost of record keeping.

Being able to describe exactly the distinguishing characteristics of a base unit provides difficulties. In most cases it is necessary to create a list of property record items, assigned asset categories, and classifications. These are documented in the asset manual and are available for all who must produce asset documents. Documenting new purchases that are not yet included on these lists requires the involvement of the asset manager or accountant.

These difficulties can be overcome by having the asset manager and accountant create lists of base units, assign property record classification, and include each item in the asset manual.

Policies established for capitalization and accounting for assets must be documented. Consistency in applying these policies is necessary to have meaningful records that allow for good asset management. The documentation of these policies is covered in Chapter 6, "Asset Policies Manual."

Establishing policies that define the base unit within the property record can have a major impact on consistency. For example, a building can be constructed as a shell with only bearing walls and permanent fixtures installed at time of construction. As each occupant moves in, they purchase drapes, blinds, and rugs and install walls, counters, and partitions. This method would have a different accounting treatment than if the building were constructed as a "turnkey" operation. When the construction project includes all elements of making the building ready to occupy, everything is included in the initial building capitalization.

Establishing base units reduces this problem and provides for a consistent property record being constructed under either scenario. Each of the major components of the building should be established as a base unit when it is valued at more than $1,000 and has a life expectancy beyond two years. Smaller, less expensive items should be included in a larger base unit. The base units will be the same if installed during the building construction phase added later.

The following sections explore the example of a building, the base units to be established, and the policies that should define them.

LAND

Each separate parcel of land should be established as a separate base unit. If a parcel has a separate property tax bill from the taxing agency, it should have its own property record. However, parcels can vary from a small lot to one that is thousands of acres in size. Included within the base unit of a land parcel are the costs of clearing and preparing the land for use. Permanent drainage facilities as well as utility improvements for sewer communications and power are included within the land base unit. However, improvements such as parking lots, landscaping, and sprinkler systems where the value is greater than $1,000 should be separate base units in the building account. Each base unit will be separately recorded as an asset and a property record will be maintained. Items that require monitoring for appropriate maintenance and replacement should be included as a separate base unit and property record item. The land account should not include items that are subject to regular maintenance or replacement.

BUILDINGS

In establishing a base unit for buildings, thought must be given to whether each individual building is maintained separately or if auxiliary structures are to be part of the basic building. Generally, it is appropriate for each building to be a separate base unit. However, where a large building exists with an adjacent ancillary structure, such as for power or grounds maintenance storage, the two structures could be included as one. In reviewing the building, however, it must be kept in mind that the building structure with routine painting and maintenance will last indefinitely. However, components of that building such as heating, air conditioning, roofs, gutters, and drainage have a more finite life. When addressing the establishment of one base unit for the entire structure as opposed to having the roof or heating system as a separate base unit, look at the accounting that will occur over the life of the building as a result of establishing base units.

After the building has been in place for some time, maintenance and modifications to its systems will be necessary. If a new roof is required, is it appropriate to retire the old one and capitalize the new one? Accounting practices call for retirement and recapitalization if it substantially increases the value of the asset or extends its life. The same is true with painting the structure. However, normal wear and tear of the building will probably require some rooms to be painted on an annual basis. It is general practice to repaint offices and rooms when they are vacated due to a change of occupant. This does not extend the life of the building, however it is less expensive to paint an empty room, and new occupants generally have their own pictures and appointments that do not always hide the scars of the previous tenant.

When a heating or cooling motor or compressor needs replacement, is this routine maintenance or is it the replacement of a major item that should be capitalized?

The desirable outcome of the accounting policy is to ensure that the costs of assets and their maintenance be accounted for on a consistent basis and recovered from the periods that benefitted from their use. It is also appropriate to keep records in an economic fashion. If every small item that was replaced in a building required capitalization and the original item retired, little benefit would occur to the management of the business, however, accounting costs would be increased. The purpose for establishing and documenting policies is to allow different people to arrive at the same accounting classification faced with similar facts.

Instead of capitalization and retirement of every item, establishing a consistent policy of base units allows the replacement of anything less than a base unit to be done on an expense basis. Therefore if the entire roof is established as the base unit, its replacement would be done on a retirement and capitalization basis. Similarly, with the heating and cooling unit, if the compressor or motor is a component of the heating system base unit, it would be expensed when replaced. This would be true even if the component and compressor had lives in excess of two years and a value greater than $1,000. The rationale for expensing these components is that the total building is made up of numerous systems and on average each year of its total life, maintenance will be necessary. Although not the same cost, for each accounting period on average over the life of the asset its cost will approximate what would have occurred with each individual item capitalized and retired.

To fully understand this example, we might look at a building built in 1990. It is reinforced, poured-concrete construction with metal door frames, doors, and windows. This basic structure will require little maintenance other than painting over the years. It will be established as a base unit. Another base unit is the roof, which, with our present construction techniques, will probably require major maintenance every ten years, with replacement in total at twenty to twenty-five years. Where tile or slate roofs are used, as in Europe, it will have a life as long as the building structure and be included in the building base unit. Rugs on the floors are separate base units and will require replacement every five to seven years. Paint on the building itself will be included as part of the building structure unit. The outside of the building, being basic concrete, will not require routine maintenance. However, the landscaping around a park-like building will require regular weekly gardening and some removal and replacement of trees and shrubs every five to ten years. The watering system for the grounds will also deteriorate and will require monthly maintenance after the first couple of years. The parking lot and roads will require resealing and repair as they deteriorate from cold winters, wet substrata, and heavy vehicles.

If these assets are not monitored and maintenance performed on a regular basis, the facility will generally deteriorate and lose its functional ability. If, at ten years, a major renovation of the building is done, catching up on all of this maintenance, the matching principle would require that the old units be retired and the new be capitalized. If maintenance is performed on a routine basis with a small portion done annually, the maintenance and replacement of less than a base unit would be expensed as incurred. Those replacements of an entire base unit such as the replacement of a roof, would be capitalized and the original one retired. It can be seen, therefore, that the establishment of a base unit in the property record and the monitoring of its maintenance can affect accounting. By managing the asset and ensuring that maintenance occurs as it is required, there will be a fairly uniform expense over the life of the building.

EQUIPMENT

Establishing a base unit for equipment is more complicated than establishing a base unit for land or buildings. For example, take the case of a manufacturing production line. This could include a number of machines and associated conveyor structures. Each individual item can be one base unit or an entire assembly line can be considered one base unit. Policies must be written to clearly and consistently determine what a new base unit will be.

CRITERIA FOR ESTABLISHING BASE UNITS

Generally, all things that have a similar life, are acquired together, and are used together should be a single base unit. However, the ability to control the asset should be reviewed. As establishment of the base unit will affect future depreciation and capitalization versus expense decisions, the important thing is a consistent management policy. These elements must be considered in establishing the policy:

- The estimated life of the unit will be a composite of its parts
- Items of substantially dissimilar lives should not be included in the same base unit
- The minimum value should generally be $1,000
- Include items used together, such as two interconnected machines, as one base unit
- Stand-alone or equipment of substantial value should not be grouped

In a theoretical assembly line we can address each of these items and explore the impacts of the policy determined. The assembly line could consist of a roller or conveyor line bringing raw materials to a computer-guided milling machine and an associated manual finishing trimming equipment. The questions that must be asked include: Is the computer useful for any other purpose or is it dedicated to this one? In establishing the base unit common lives must be looked at first. The computer portion is likely to have a shorter life either due to obsolescence or increased maintenance costs. The milling machine may be single purpose or more likely suitable for multiple purpose. Are the dies in the machine a substantial investment relative to the remainder of the equipment? Sometimes dies require considerable engineering costs. If so, the total percentage of costs may indicate it is appropriate for the dies to be separate items.

If it is established that the milling machine and conveyors attached to it are one base unit, the finishing machine a separate base unit, and the computer a third, it is helpful to explore the accounting for maintenance to these machines over a theoretical ten-year life. Routine maintenance, oiling, adjustment, and repair of broken parts will be accomplished either on a routine schedule, after a fixed number of hours of use, or as malfunctions occur. Components of the computer, especially in a dirty environment, may require replacement more often than other items, especially key boards and other input–output devices, which are mechanical in nature and subject to wear and deterioration from dirt. If the assembly line runs two shifts a day, six days a week, with maintenance scheduled during one of those mid-week shifts and on the seventh day, a number of components within each of these base units will have been replaced over the ten-year life. All of the removable, replaceable parts on the equipment might even have been replaced, with only the frames and major components still the original parts. If over the ten-year life, one tenth of this maintenance and replacement has occurred each year (assuming equal usage each year) we will have properly matched this cost with its periods of benefit. That is the intent we should have as we establish a base unit. Creating base units of a large enough size is necessary for this to happen. Small base units increase the cost of the accounting process with little benefit.

The base unit should be:

Smallest asset unit

Property record unit

Made up of components with equal lives

Similar tax rules

Identifiable

Subject to periodic verification

EXAMPLES

The following is a list of asset categories and base unit classifications that might be included in an asset manual.

Asset Category	Base Unit
Computers	Central processing unit, disk drive, printer, monitor, back-up tape drive, keyboard, modem
Software	Operating system compiler, telecommunications software, word processor, spreadsheet
Aircraft	Airframe, engines, radio set, navigation computer, emergency oxygen, megaphone, first aid equipment, life raft, emergency slide, cargo tie downs
Light trucks	Refrigeration units, utility beds, trailer, air compressor, electric generator, hydraulic lift, hydraulic crane
Land	Landscaping, underground utilities
Building	Building shell, roof, air conditioning unit, heating unit, parking lot, elevators, escalators, plumbing, electrical wiring
Furniture	Typewriters, television, monitor, video camera, conference table
Manufacturing equipment	Milling machine, conveyor, computer operating system

SPARE PARTS

Normally, spare parts are expensed when purchased or, if significant, are kept in a supplies account and expensed as used. However, where expensive parts such as circuit boards for electronics equipment must be maintained, it may be appropriate to capitalize them as part of the unit in service. An example would be a local area network containing a number of personal computers. If ten computers are in service, an additional maintenance space may be maintained. The space is capitalized on the property record. Location code can indicate an availability.

5

CONTROL OF PROPERTY, PLANT, AND EQUIPMENT

INTRODUCTION

The concepts of total quality management and zero defects must be included in management of assets. The quality of the final product, be it a manufactured item or the services of a bank or accounting firm, will be directly related to the emphasis placed on managing physical assets.

Providing adequate control of property, plant, and equipment can take many forms. In the past, the control system for assets has been to have the external auditor produce a balance sheet certified as meeting generally accepted accounting principles. The many disasters where assets listed on the balance sheet did not have the value stated, have caused a necessity for rethinking this approach. The responsibility for an internal control system rests with the company management. The purpose of an external audit is to make tests only to ensure that, in all probability, the intent of the management control system has been carried out. Controls, to be effective, must be part of the day-to-day management of the firm.

Why are controls necessary? The possibility of loss, of course, is ever present. Equipment can be misplaced, or misappropriated for other than the purposes of the business. An even greater possibility for loss is the deterioration of equipment because it has not been properly maintained. The future cost of a disruption of business due to breakdown of equipment can be considerable. A technically inferior process can also result in a reduction of the quality of product. This can be seen in the steel industry where the furnaces and equipment that produced steel in the 1930s and 1940s began to decline in quality in the 1950s and beyond. Only with a complete replacement and building of new plants can the quality of U.S. steel meet the requirements of today.

Control also has to do with ensuring that the best use is made of assets. If a ten-ton truck is used for a one-ton job, that is not the best use of the assets. Management must provide procedures that, if followed, will ensure that assets are used to their maximum and to the benefit of the organization. They must have a plan in place to provide for required maintenance of the equipment. Management must also provide plans and budgets for replacement and necessary additional acquisitions.

Controls need to be in place to ensure that someone is aware of underutilized resources, which can be reallocated or transferred to avoid the cost of purchasing new ones. Both the cost of physical assets and the cost of maintaining debt to finance these assets have increased dramatically.

In order to manage a profitable business, the management must have information regarding the current location, use, state of repair, and future usefulness of its productive assets. The chief financial officer has a duty to ensure a system is in place to provide this information. However, creating this system is not just an accounting, it will require the assistance and time of other senior managers. An asset control system consists of all the elements of capital budgeting, property record maintenance, maintenance review, and management performance appraisal.

Asset control processes must be documented in the asset manual and have the support of senior management.

ASSET ACCOUNTANT

The asset accountant will ensure that a capital budget is produced and approved. This is the future plan for purchases of physical assets. The purchasing authority will be verified on each requisition. Overruns of capital budgets will be brought to the attention of the involved managers. This task of providing reports to management and asset custodians is the most important task of the asset accountant. The reporting system should provide the means to make management aware when their action is required. Asset accounting will be a full-time function in most businesses. However, the asset custodian and department managers have many functions to accomplish. Therefore, the information provided them should include exception reports.

Reports on Proper Asset Utilization

Production assets should have a means of determining hours or miles of usage. Reports that produce the number of miles per month vehicles travel or hours of usage for buildings and other production equipment provide a means to make comparisons. Assets that have very low usage should be brought to the attention of custodians and managers. Perhaps such equipment should be sold and replaced by rented equipment if used for only small periods of time. Perhaps additional functions can be moved to property that is underutilized. By adding to this information a record of past maintenance expense, a forecast can be made as to the requirements for replacement.

A comparison of maintenance expense by individual item to past maintenance expense, as well as in total to the maintenance budget can identify potential problems. A periodic assessment of the state of maintenance of production assets will identify the deferred maintenance that exists.

ASSET CUSTODIAN

Each department manager should assign an asset custodian. This need not be a full-time position, but it must be a significant part of the custodian's performance measurement. If asset management and control is a once-a-year assessment, it will never be effective. Procedures must be put in place to hold the department manager and the asset custodian responsible for the proper utilization of assets in their areas.

Responsibility for the maintenance of asset records and their location must be measured.

Each asset custodian will receive a monthly report of new acquisitions. The custodian must verify the accuracy of the information, ensure the item has been placed in use, and affix inventory tags as appropriate. This monthly report should be a turnaround document, which goes back to the accounting and inventory management so they may update the file. Although the requisition to purchase the item will have included much of the information, it may not have included all. For example, a new motor vehicle will not have its state-issued license number on the requisition. This must be added, together with the vehicle's specific location, and other required information which is known to the asset custodian.

INVENTORIES

On a periodic basis, complete verification of the existence and state of assets must occur. For many assets, this should occur on an annual basis. However, verification should also occur at the time a department manager or custodian is assigned. This action emphasizes responsibility for proper use and maintenance of the assets assigned. It also eliminates future disagreements as to who might have been responsible for asset deteriorization. Many companies have adopted this "military commander" procedure for ensuring proper stewardship of assets assigned to managers. The inventory record of property is maintained within the controller's department. However, the responsibility for accuracy and proper reporting stays with the manager utilizing the property, plant, and equipment.

The military approach works well because fully ingrained in the officer effectiveness review process is the need for asset stewardship. Each military commander has assigned a trained supply officer whose career is dependent on ensuring that assets are maintained and used to their fullest. An incoming unit commander is responsible for reviewing and signing off on the assets he or she will control.

It has been common practice in the past for U.S. industry to be concerned only about the location, existence, and condition of production assets when they breakdown or at the time of an annual inventory. It has not been unusual for significant assets to be written off and later found and added back to the record in this annual process.

By emphasizing the stewardship responsibility of each manager and using the records in the day-to-day management of the business, many of these problems can be overcome.

PROPERTY RECORD SYSTEM

Chapter 12 outlines in detail the production of an asset property record as an integral part of the general ledger system. Refer to Chapter 12 for the details of the system. In this section, how to ensure that the asset property record is part of the control system will also be discussed.

To be part of an internal control system, the property record must not stand alone as something unique. When a requisition to purchase is processed, it should create the accounts payable record as well as the initial property record entry. Similarly, maintenance records of individual assets should not be a separate report. Either the employee time report or the invoice for paying a maintenance firm should generate the proper record for payment and record the dollar amount of that maintenance within the property record system. The reports of asset location and utilization should be aggregated for the entire department and company. By including within the review of senior management comparisons of utilization records, proper recognition will be given to those managers with the best records. Capturing the information for the reports from normal required reporting and not the creation of a separate document will eliminate many reconciliation problems and considerably improve accuracy.

The time report of the maintenance employee has a direct impact on his paycheck. By using that time report for property record updating, no separate verification or reconciliation is necessary. It is self-policing. Verification and reconciliation steps are not value added, only overhead.

IDENTIFICATION OF ASSETS

Some means of identifying the item and to whom it belongs needs to be established. There are a number of ways to accomplish this. Individual equipment tags can show the name of the company. The company name may also be stenciled or painted on the equipment. Sometimes special color schemes are used to identify ownership, as military vehicles use unique paint colors.

Company name may not, however, be sufficient to identify ownership. Some industries have established special identification systems.

FARM OWNER APPLIED NUMBERS

There is a specific problem with portable farm equipment that has all the characteristics of motor vehicles, such as automobiles and trucks, but which is not licensed by a government entity. The problems with misplacing or theft of such equipment and a need for law enforcement identification has brought about a system called farm owner applied numbers.

The numbering system was developed by law enforcement in cooperation with the American Farm Bureau. It includes the first two letters of the state name, a three digit county identifier, and the individual business or ranch number. For example:

CA 049 0110 P

CA is the post office identifier for the State of California.

049 is a three-digit identifier for Sonoma County, one of fifty-eight counties in California.

0110 is the unique number issued sequentially to the agricultural business requesting a number through its law enforcement agency or farm bureau.

P is a letter used as a control digit.

The farm bureau lends both metal stamp kits for pounding into metal objects and rubber stamps with difficult-to-remove ink for application of the number on all owned property.

Companies may also acquire a specific kit for their own use.

The number is readily identified by law enforcement officers so that if they should find a piece of equipment with the number applied, they have the means of tracing it back to the owner in the same fashion as a state vehicle license number.

This type of an identification system provides a positive means of tracing the owner. Of course, it comes about as a result of long years of difficulty identifying ownership of property that has been commingled. The concept of burning the owner's initial or brand into young animals is ancient. Registering brands and assigning a specific place on the animal makes the establishment of ownership fairly easy. Prior to the establishment of the owner identification system in agricultural businesses, a popular technique was to use the owner's individual driver's license number. The stamping, etching, or printing of the Department of Motor Vehicles-assigned driver's license number of the owner may be a reasonable way for small businesses to identify their equipment.

Stenciling the firm name on an item to be sold may also be done for advertising purposes. Others may not recognize the difference between your name and that of a manufacturer; therefore, it does not serve to prove ownership.

These systems provide ownership identification. That is all that is necessary for many items. Chairs in a conference room need not be individually identified. However, small expensive items such as computers or works of art require a means of specific identification.

IDENTIFICATION OF SPECIFIC ASSET

If you have more than one asset of an identical nature, how will you determine who the custodian is of that particular asset? Its location may make it obvious if it is in a building with a specific address. However, items of value that are movable should be identified with an individual specific number. Otherwise, it is not possible to maintain a property record by individual item. See Chapter 4, "Establishment of a Base Unit," to determine what to tag.

Each individual base unit should have affixed its own unique identification number. These numbers should be preprinted on an easily affixed, but difficult to remove, substance. Many companies manufacture such tags and will print your company name at little additional cost. These tags should be controlled by the asset accountant or a series of them should be assigned to departmental asset custodians. This unique number needs to be on the piece of equipment and reported with each transaction that is to be captured on property record file. This number will be the property record key. In the mechanized property record, that unique number is what will identify the asset involved.

Tagging of each item makes its identification for periodic inventories simple. These tags can be bar coded. This provides the means for their being read by a small reading wand and recorded on a portable computer input device.

The individual identification number on the tag provides positive identification between specific valuable items, such as laboratory equipment, expensive portable tools, personal computers, or medical devices.

The individual tag number reported by maintenance personnel on their time reports allows the capturing of the cost of that main-

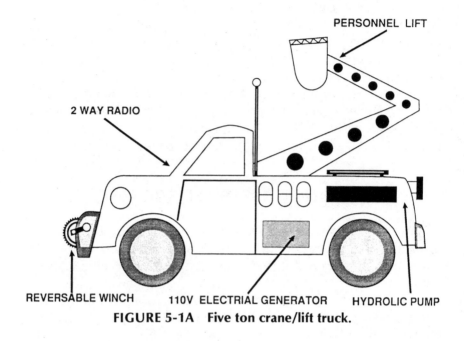

FIGURE 5-1A   Five ton crane/lift truck.

tenance in the accounting system. The individual custodian of the equipment can be readily identified by the tag number. It provides the means of communication between asset users, their departmental custodian, the asset accountant, and the property record system.

ITEMS TO BE TAGGED

All items that are to be individually controlled must have separate serial numbers and tags. If items such as folding chairs or office equipment are not to be individually controlled, they do not require individual tags. This decision should be made in the establishment of a base unit and property record item. Similarly, items that have been expensed because they are inexpensive, but are to be main-

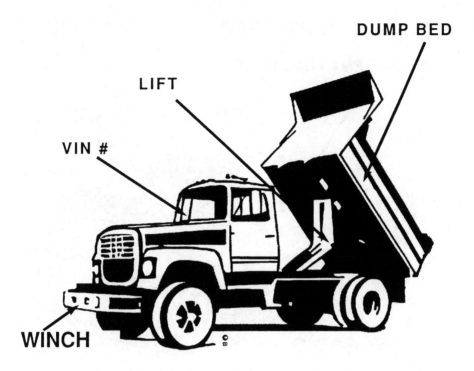

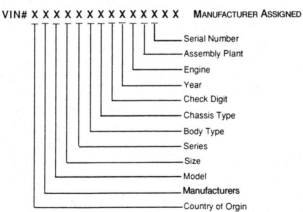

FIGURE 5-1B   10 ton dump truck.

PROPERTY RECORD NUMBERS

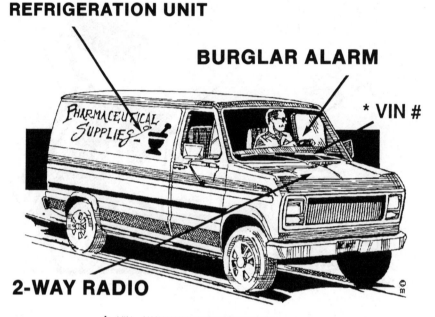

REFRIGERATION UNIT

BURGLAR ALARM

* VIN #

2-WAY RADIO

★ VIN = XXXXXXXXXXXXXXXX

FIGURE 5-1C   2 ton delivery van.

tained on the property record for some reason, should be tagged. Examples of expensed items might be portable video cameras with a value of less than $1,000. Although expensed, they are subject to loss and may require more detailed controls. In hospitals or ambulances, pieces of medical equipment such as defibrillators need to be controlled as to location and proper preventive maintenance. As these electronic devices cost less than $1,000, they are expensed for accounting purposes, but require property record control and therefore should be individually numbered and tagged.

An auditorium full of portable chairs may require property record keeping to establish business property tax or insurance value. The tagging of individual items may not be necessary if the base unit is established as a room full of furniture and a number assigned for property record purposes accordingly. The number assigned to a

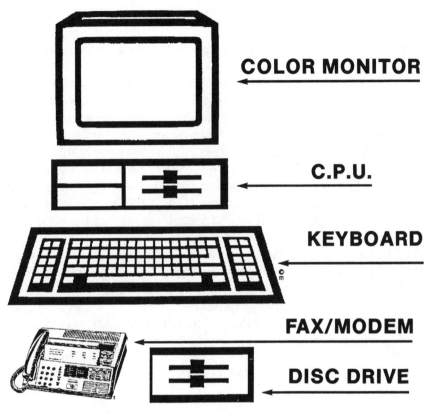

FIGURE 5-1D   Personal computer (PC).

record may contain a description as "100 meeting room chairs." The building number and room number may establish both the location and the correlation to a property record number. There is little risk in terms of deferred maintenance or disruption of the business if these chairs are lost or deteriorate. Their disappearance would be conspicuous. Therefore, if the locale of the business does not require a business property tax on the value of such furniture, the company may elect not to tag or control them at all. Such chairs may be excluded from property records and efforts reduced.

There is also little risk if they are moved to another location, because the users and custodian would be aware of their disappearance.

BAR CODED TAGS

Bar coding of individual asset tags will significantly reduce the efforts necessary for inventories. With portable computer input devices the size of a small tape recorder, it is possible to quickly conduct an inventory. Upon entering a building, the personnel taking the inventory enter the building number into the device, then enter each floor and room number as they go through the building. As they pass each individual asset item, they run the bar code reader, which is the size of a large fountain pen, over the tag. This establishes positively the presence of that tag, and its associated item, in the location inventory. The computer, upon reading the input information, can identify items that have changed locations and produce an exception list. The bar code reader eliminates the problems of transcription errors on the part of a human reading a number and either keying or writing it on a document. Pre-numbered, bar coded tags including your company name, can be obtained from many firms specializing in inventory equipment.

For a business with more than a few hundred assets, bar coding is highly recommended.

SECURITY

Items of high value, which may be converted to other uses, need additional security measures. Items may be taken for personal use or sold by employees, customers, or others. Maintaining the property record is the first necessity of any security system in order to establish the fact that an item did exist. Assigning a custodian so that someone is responsible to regularly check on its existence is the second necessity. An item that is found may be traced back to its custodian. Similarly, any item that cannot be found will have an audit trail back to the last assigned custodian.

In addition to this, tagging and identification reduce probability of misuse. However, procedures for periodic inventories, requirements for approval for removal from the premises, donation, and destruction of no longer needed items must be included in the asset accounting manual.

Management must maintain an attitude of protection of the company's assets. An attitude that "we spend too much time" on inventories leads to poor security procedures. The axiom in an audit process of "assume everyone is honest, but do not allow anyone to be otherwise" should be followed. Procedures should be such that if expensive equipment is removed, it will be missed within a reasonable time, and some record will exist as to who had access during that period.

Also, it should be kept in mind that loss is not always due to theft; it may occur in the normal course of activities. A library book misfiled on the shelf will only be found by accident in the future. A defibrillator removed from an ambulance and left at an accident scene will never be found if it is not missed immediately. Typically, in such a rescue vehicle, an inventory is taken at the beginning of each shift. The new crew verifies that all of the equipment is present, restocks any disposable items, and enters that information in the record. Such procedures should be established on some basis with all expensive convertible assets. In a manufacturing plant, expensive tools for milling equipment that are used sporadically should be controlled individually. The tools should be locked in a special cabinet with a record listing who removed them and when they were replaced. Items that are used every day in the production process would not require such control because they would be missed immediately.

Procedures for security should, wherever possible, be integrated with the normal functions of those using the items. In the example of the inventory at the beginning of a new emergency ambulance crew shift, it is not just for equipment security. The crew needs to ensure that they are adequately stocked and that all equipment is in working order. The start up of an assembly line can provide a similar status report. The review of each equipment item as to its proper condition before starting the line, can be constructed to provide a positive inventory report as well as an assessment of future maintenance requirements. During pre-flight checks, the crew of an airliner notes any missing items or minor maintenance deficiencies. Missing items or serious maintenance deficiencies require "grounding" the aircraft.

Similar procedures should be established for large equipment operators and can be adapted for laboratories, research and development facilities, and service organizations.

Failing to provide procedures for the control and security of movable assets implies a reduced level of concern.

The purpose of checking out books from a library is to provide a means of tracing the books if they are not returned; but greater than that, it is to remind the person using the items that they are to be returned on time.

Procedures should be documented and followed, including the conditions under which property may be borrowed for employees' personal use. Many firms specifically forbid personal use.

Surplus and/or obsolete equipment should be identified quickly and normal procedures for disposing of it followed. Equipment that is no longer used can get lost in the process very quickly. The handling of such surplus can telegraph management's concern over asset management to the entire organization. If material is quickly identified as surplus, placed in use elsewhere, or disposed of according to written procedures, it avoids the breeding of bad attitudes. If the opposite occurs and surplus property is in the way until it just disappears, employees grow indifferent to company property. The most important element of property record, security, and control is to have written procedures that are so simple and so much a part of the users' job routine that they are followed.

6

ASSET POLICIES MANUAL

INTRODUCTION

The many policies and procedures regarding tangible physical assets outlined in this book must be documented for each business. A procedures manual may be developed for your entire accounting process. In that case, tangible assets or property, plant, and equipment will be one of its sub-parts. In this chapter the manual will be discussed as if it were a separate, stand-alone document.

PURPOSE

Documenting the policies and procedures that have been established will save considerable time in the day-to-day coding of transactions. Included within the manual should be instructions necessary for:

1. Gathering the needed physical asset accounting information
2. Coding the information
3. Reporting that information

The written instructions necessary to provide a thorough understanding of the asset and property record process should also be included. This information should be written in a manner that will be understandable by both accountants and nonfinancial employees. Therefore, the use of jargon and other accounting-related terms should be kept to a minimum. Any accounting terms that are used must be defined.

Chapters 1 through 5 of this book explained how to make many of the decisions that the asset accountant or manager must make in establishing a physical asset accounting system. The purpose of this chapter is to outline the documentation of the decisions the asset accountant makes for the organization. It is important to make those decisions and document them in a fashion that can be used by the entire organization. Each person who is involved in the acquisition, payment for, or receipt of physical property needs to know how to code and report the transaction.

The amount of effort made in establishing and documenting an accounting system can considerably reduce the day-to-day effort by others. The asset accountant must identify and code the many standard transactions that will occur. The employee creating a purchase order for a new truck or equipment should then be able to look up the correct coding within the accounting manual and apply it to the proper transaction document.

Similarly, the employee responsible for maintaining these items should be able to find the instructions necessary for reporting maintenance. The simpler and more automatic the reporting is within the system, the better will be the quality of the data within your property record. The responsibilities of the property accountant must be described, and the responsibility and authority of physical property custodians must be established as well.

Disposition of physical assets is an important part of the internal control system for the organization. The authority to approve the disposition of assets should be clearly outlined: How should these assets be disposed of? Are they to be sent to a central location for determination if they can be used elsewhere, or is it up to the discretion of the asset custodian? Large organizations should have some regular means of communicating the availability of furniture, computer components, conveyor belts, and other equipment that may be of use elsewhere in the organization. Periodic communication between physical asset custodians, listing available materials, might be sufficient for smaller organizations.

There should be an established procedure and means of approval for the disposition of any physical asset. Generally, in the case of land or buildings, someone with real estate disposition responsibility will conduct a sale. When worn out or no longer useful material is to be disposed of, procedures should be established as to who may decide to junk, donate, or conduct some means of sale of the item.

CREATING THE MANUAL

In order to produce the accounting manual, it is necessary to establish a clear understanding of the accounting system within the organization. You should examine unwritten policies and procedures that exist so that they can be documented also. If an existing manual outlines procedures, do not expect that it contains all the information you need. As a practical matter, most employees probably have some informal process of obtaining the appropriate coding for transactions. They will have the numbers written down and put them on every transaction that comes along until they are told differently. Most will rarely code a transaction for a physical asset. Therefore, special care must be made to index the manual in a manner that provides easy access to the information needed.

Creation of the asset accounting manual can be done during a specified time frame. However, it is going to be necessary to dedicate someone to do the writing. If the writer is also involved in daily production activities, it will reduce the quality of the product as well as extend the time to accomplish it. Once the manual has been written, the persons involved can be reassigned. However, there will be ongoing revisions to the manual. It is important that the manual be updated as new types of items are utilized within the company. As questions are referred to the asset manager or accountant, the decisions made should be documented within the manual. This revision can be accomplished by someone, such as an asset accountant, as a part-time activity. The partial sample that follows provides an example of a manual.

PARTIAL SAMPLE MANUAL

TABLE OF CONTENTS

Manufacturer Serial Number
Manufacturer Warranty Date
Manufacturer Acquisition Date
Location Code
Source Code
Tax Code
    Real Estate
    Business Property Tax
Insurance Class
Department Code
Custodian
Life Expectancy
    Accounting Depreciation Life
    Tax Depreciation Life
Leased Assets
    Monthly Lease Fee
    Lease End Date
Work Order Number
Vehicle License Number
    Relicense Date
State Inspection Due Date
Date Placed in Service
Date of Addition
Retirement Code
    Disposal—Date; Method; Proceeds
Original Cost
Reproduction Cost, New
Insurance Value
Current Market Price

This manual is to be used by all members of the organization to outline procedures for coding transactions that affect property record items. The codes necessary to report the transactions, as well as the documents and computer processes to be used are contained in this manual. It provides one source for obtaining the information you need. If you use the information in this manual to determine the coding of asset transactions, there will be accurate consistent accounting information.

USE OF THE MANUAL

All of the accounting coding systems for physical items are outlined in the manual. The table of contents or the index may be consulted to find a specific transaction type.

PROPERTY, PLANT, AND EQUIPMENT
CUSTODIAN'S RESPONSIBILITIES

Each department manager has assigned a custodian for the property, plant, and equipment used by the organization. The individual assigned as custodian is responsible for the property records. The asset accountant will manage the overall property record system and is available to assist. However, each departmental asset custodian is responsible for the accuracy of the property records. This includes:

1. Reporting any change in location
2. Planning and obtaining proper maintenance
3. Creating the annual capital budget for the department
4. Ensuring that a plan exists for replacements of worn-out equipment.

The custodian will receive monthly reports of new property, plant, and equipment acquisitions for the department. He or she should verify the accuracy of the information and ensure that the item has been placed in use. It is also necessary to complete the forms to update all information in the property record for new acquisitions.

Annually, a verification and estimate of deferred maintenance is required. The asset accountant will ensure the creation of this report. He or she will send it to the custodian together with a due date for its return so that property records can be updated prior to the time budgets that must be produced.

Inventories of all property, plant, and equipment within the department will be completed by the custodian or under his or her direction on an annual basis in conjunction with the verification and estimate of deferred maintenance, and additionally, whenever either the department manager or the custodian is reassigned.

As part of the total quality management program, strive to produce products that have zero defects. It is very important that proper planning and control of the assets used in production be accomplished. The management of property, plant, and equipment is not simply maintaining an accounting record. It also involves ensuring that these items are maintained in a proper manner so as to produce quality products with minimal disruption of production.

RESPONSIBILITIES OF ASSET ACCOUNTANT

The asset accountant is responsible for the overall management and control of the property records system. He or she will establish procedures to assist all department custodians in accomplishing their responsibilities. Whenever a custodian has a problem or question he or she cannot address, it should be referred to the property accountant.

The updating of the asset accounting manual will be accomplished by the asset accountant. Suggestions for updates and changes are encouraged from all personnel using it.

The reports necessary to accomplish the updates to the property record system will be created and distributed to custodians and their department managers by the asset accountant.

The overall management of the annual inventory including verification of existence, location and proper utilization and assessment of maintenance requirements for all property, plant, and equipment will be directed by the asset accountant. Whenever a department manager or custodian is reassigned, reports will be issued by the new manager or custodian to verify the status of all property, plant, and equipment.

Specific duties of the asset accountant include:

- Verification of purchase authority for each asset requisition
- Review of the capital budget to ensure large purchase items were previously included
- Review overruns of capital budget with the department manager involved and the Audit Committee of the Board of Directors

- Manage the accounting for internally constructed items, making sure all appropriate costs are included
- Make reports of any abandoned construction and ensure proper accounting
- Maintain quality control reports for both self-constructed and purchased asset items
- Provide necessary reports to both management and custodians. They must be made aware when their action is required for proper asset maintenance
- Produce reports on an exception basis providing:
  Verification of proper asset utilization
  Periodic maintenance expense incurred, including exceptions to the maintenance budget
  Annual and quarterly reports of cumulative deferred maintenance on production assets
  Forecast replacements based on age, past maintenance experience, and assessment of future maintenance needs

PROCEDURES FOR PURCHASE OF PHYSICAL ASSETS

The purchase of individual items of value greater than $1,000 or group purchases more than $5,000 must be approved in advance in the capital budget. Those identifying the need for such purchases should notify the departmental custodian for inclusion on the next capital budget. Where emergencies that have not been included in the current budget occur, the custodian will ask for approval by the departmental manager and the budget committee.

The responsible manager will notify purchasing with sufficient lead time to produce a requisition to be approved by the departmental custodian, asset accountant, and appropriate manager.

APPROVAL LIMITS

Items that have already been included on the capital expenditure budget may be approved by the ordering manager if less than $5,000 each. Purchases of items greater than $5,000 must be referred to the department manager for approval. Purchases of items in excess of $25,000 must be approved by the budget committee.

Approval for transfers of assets from one custodian to another for items less than $5,000 is by the receiving custodian. For items greater than $5,000, approval of the receiving department manager is required. Transfer of custodial responsibility for items in excess of $100,000 aggregate will require approval by the chairman of the capital budget committee.

Final approval for dispositions of less than $1,000 will be by the responsible manager and asset custodian. Donations or junking of assets with an estimated value of greater than $25,000 will be approved by the department manager. All dispositions of real estate will be approved by the chairman of the budget committee and the controller.

MINIMUM CAPITALIZATION LEVEL

All individual purchases of $5,000 or more will be capitalized. Also, any group purchases of similar items that in aggregate amount to $5,000 or more are to be capitalized. This would include such items as folding chairs or other furniture items normally expensed. The asset manager should be contacted to obtain appropriate group property record codes for these items.

Individual items purchased for less than $5,000 will be charged to departmental expense accounts and are not included in the capital budget allocation or approval process. However, individual items classifiable to the general ledger accounts for office equipment—computers, aircraft, light trucks, land, or buildings—that cost more than $1,000 will be capitalized. Other items that are identified as a separate base unit with property record numbers assigned will be charged to capital accounts.

Care must be taken in classifying items to the appropriate accounts. Questions should be referred to the asset accountant.

ITEMS ALWAYS CHARGED TO EXPENSE ACCOUNT

Individual items that do not have a property record number assigned will always be charged to an expense account if purchased for less than $5,000. Items that are components of larger items not having a specifically assigned property record number will be charged to expense no matter what the purchase price. However, any individual item costing more than $5,000 should be referred to the asset accountant to ensure proper approvals and coding occurs.

Furniture items purchased for less than an entire office will be expensed.

TRANSACTION REPORTS

Whoever takes the action to purchase, transfer, or dispose of any property, plant, or equipment, must fill out the appropriate property record form to record that transaction. When completed and approved, the form is forwarded to the property record accountant for processing.

Special emphasis must be placed on transfer and disposition reports. Only those involved in the transaction will be aware of its occurrence unless the report is completed. Failure to report a transfer can cause the property custodian considerable difficulty at the next inventory. Items that are retired or transferred from a department continue to be included in the investment base upon which the department is measured until the appropriate form is received and processed in the property record system.

Maintenance of items of property, plant, or equipment that contain individual identification tags should include the property record number on their maintenance time report. This allows proper record keeping of the cumulative maintenance occurring on various property record items. This report of maintenance time ensures that information will be available to determine when items requiring excessive maintenance should be replaced.

DATA DEFINITIONS

Classification and assignment of codes to transactions is the way to communicate with the asset database. The codes assigned will be stored in database field. The definition and purpose of these data fields are:

General Ledger Account

A six-digit numeric code which identifies the general ledger asset account.

General Ledger Depreciation Expense Account

This is the expense account to which the depreciation charged for these items will be coded.

Property Type

This field is used to indicate whether an asset for tax purposes is real, personal, leased, historical, low income housing, or other property. This field will be used to allow income tax calculation of the alternative minimum tax. Distinguishing between personal property will allow proper calculation and preparation of personal property tax reports. Any question on the assignment of this code should be referred to the property record accountant or the tax department.

Asset Identification Number

This six-digit field will be assigned sequentially by the property record accountant during the approval for purchase process. It will be included on the purchase order and all subsequent documents pertaining to this property record item. It is the primary key for identifying and accessing the record for a specific property record item. Tags will be sent to the department custodian for attachment to the property record item displaying this number.

Description of Asset

This field contains the English language description of the property record item. The standard descriptions included in the appendices should be used where provided. Note that the manufacturer's name is not necessary as it is included in a separate field. Care should be taken to use the same descriptions for identical items. Although this field is not used for property record accounting purposes, the inventory reports produced will print this field. That will make it easier to locate and identify the item if standard nomenclature is used.

Vendor

This field identifies the vendor from whom the item was purchased.

Purchase Order Number

This field identifies the number of the purchase order on which this item was ordered.

Manufacturer

This is the name of the manufacturer of the item.

Manufacturer Serial Number

This identifies the serial number of the item assigned by the manufacturer. Care must be taken that this is the serial number of the base unit involved. Manufacturers may assign serial numbers to component parts of a complete item. For example, automobile manufacturers place a vehicle identification number on a plate on the body of a vehicle; that is the serial number that should be included in this field. They also include serial numbers on component parts of engines, transmissions, etc. As these items are not base units in our property record system, they will not be recorded. However, where component parts of an assembly line are each base units, the serial number of each item will be associated with its property record.

Warranty Date

This is the expiration date of the manufacturer and vendor's warranty on this item. Care should be taken to ensure this date is accurately entered. A report will be issued two months prior to the expiration date alerting maintenance to review any continuing problems with the item. A final test and report back to the vendor of any reccurring maintenance problem should occur prior to the expiration of the warranty.

Acquisition Date

This is the date that the item was actually acquired. Normally, this is the shipping date or date received if no shipping date is provided.

Location Code

This is the address and room number where the item is installed, used, or normally stored.

Source Code

This field identifies a source of the property record item.

N = purchased new from vendor
U = purchased used
T = transferred from affiliated company
M = manufactured from components

Tax Code

This field identifies the tax jurisdiction for real and personal property. California contains many overlapping jurisdictions (i.e., state, county, and city). The tax department maintains maps showing the tax code area of each of the company's locations. Appropriate codes are listed in the appendix.

Insurance Class

This field identifies the appropriate insurance category of the item. The codes identify the type of insurance, co-insurance, or self-insurance that normally pertains. Changes to this code will be made only to correct errors. Changes in assignment of insurance class during the life of the property are to be made only by the risk management department. Classification codes are:

R = Real Estate

E = Processing Equipment

MV = Motor Vehicle

Department Code

This field contains the identification code of the department using or responsible for the property record item.

Custodian

This is the name of the departmental custodian responsible for the maintenance of the property record for this item.

Life Expectancy

These fields contain the expected life in use of the item and the tax life. The tax life will be generated by the property record system based on current tax laws and the property record number. No entry is necessary.

Leased Assets

These fields contain the information regarding the lease, including the monthly lease payment amount and end of lease effective date. Department custodians will be notified prior to the end of the lease so that alternative action can be taken.

Work Order Number

Self-constructed items will contain the work order number that they were constructed under.

Vehicle License Number

The state- or county-issued vehicle license number.

Relicense Date

The calendar month that the vehicle re-registration is due. Two months prior to this date, the departmental custodian will be sent a vehicle re-registration list. Not all of the jurisdictions send annual bills for registration. It is the custodian's responsibility to ensure that the vehicle is re-registered prior to the expiration date. Failure to do so will incur penalties to the company.

State Inspection Due Date

This is the date of the next periodic inspection. Motor vehicles located in all states except California must be taken annually to a state authorized inspection station prior to registration renewal. California does not require an annual inspection, however, depending on the class of the vehicle, all vehicles must receive a smog emissions inspection on a two- or three-year basis. This field should include the date of the next smog inspection entered by the vehicle maintenance department.

Date Placed in Service

This is the date the item had all of its acceptance tests completed and is actually available to be used for company purposes. The assembly and testing of all items should occur as quickly as possible after receipt. Some manufacturers and vendors begin the warranty period as of the date of receipt. Others, notably computer manufacturers, generally begin the warranty on the date the item is placed in service and the warranty registration is filed.

Date of Addition

Where the item contains components that are also base units, this entry indicates the date that the last item was added. Examples are computer central processing units where the hard disk drives are associated component parts. The component in this case is a separate base unit with its own property record number and record.

Retirement Code

This field contains the code identifying the date, means of disposal, and salvage amount.

Original Cost

This is the total amount for the purchase price and subsequent cost necessary to make the item ready for use. Although this will normally be the invoice and shipping cost of the item, complex installations add to that cost. Production equipment that is mounted to the floor or must be lifted by cranes onto upper floors of a building will have additional costs included. Custodians should refer questions to the property record accountant.

Reproduction Cost, New

This is the current cost of replacing the item with a currently manufactured one. This item will be updated during periodic inventories and when requested by the risk management department. This is normally the amount on which insurance for fire, theft, or other catastrophe will be based.

Insurance Value

Where risk management has determined an insurance amount different from reproduction costs new, it will include it here. Departments should be aware that in case of catastrophe, the difference between reproduction costs new, and insurance value is the deductible or co-insurance amount. Insurance premiums are reduced by insuring for less than full replacement cost. However, in case of catastrophe, the insurance proceeds will be the lesser amount.

Current Market Price

This identifies what the market value of the property is on the date specified. Periodically, this amount will be updated by the property record accountant based on an appraisal. This amount is utilized in doing analysis on the company's assets to ensure that we are using assets to the fullest and know the approximate value of the assets of the company. This amount will differ from the historical cost or book value.

Location 421 East Lansing	General Ledger		Book Value
	11000	Land	2.1 acres	$2,350,275
	11110	Improvements		521,243
	12100	Office Building		1,435,986
	12120	Heat/air system		40,841
	12136	Elevator, Pass		16,852
	13301	Computers, PC		91,628
	13302	Telephone Modems		17,253
	13308	Computer, Security		9,284
	13500	Office Furniture		172,932
	13602	Drapes		86,182
	13605	Lighting		26,183
	13811	Autos, Passenger		362,741
	13830	Trucks, Delivery		81,649
836 Lincoln			
	11000	Land	927,271 feet	421,629
	11100	Grading		0
	11120	Drainage		0
	11210	Landscaping		14,923
	11250	Utilities		0
	11270	RR Siding		0
	12102	Building, Plant		614,926
	12123	Air Conditioning		12,853

FIGURE 6.1   Property record report.

7

ESTABLISHING VALUE

INTRODUCTION

Considerable discussion has occurred recently on the subject of valuing property, plant, and equipment. There has been confusion as to the result of this discussion. Much of the confusion comes about as a result of the many different procedures there are for the valuation of property, plant, and equipment and the reasons for each.

The purpose that the value is to be used for requires a different methodology for arriving at value.

Generally accepted accounting principles require that the book value of an asset appears on the balance sheet. But there are many different values for the same object.

Examples of these different values are:

- Historical cost—the book value as GAAP defines it
- Original cost—the purchase price of the item
- Replacement cost new or insurance value—the cost to purchase the same capability today
- Current market value—the amount a willing buyer will pay for it today
- Fair market value—the price that would be paid for the item in a condemnation proceeding
- Assessed value—the basis on which it will be taxed

HISTORICAL COST

Each of the many values will be different. The reason, of course, is they have different purposes and, therefore, different procedures for establishing them. These values must be determined with care and deliberation. Historical cost, or book value, is the cost of purchasing and putting an object into use. How to ascertain book value is outlined in Chapter 2, "What Is an Asset?" Most of this book covers the procedures that must be followed to ensure that historical cost meets the principles outlined.

Historical land value, once established, rarely changes and then only because of specific occurrences. Events that will change historical land value are limited to:

adding an item of significant value

extraordinary modifications or repairs that increase the value, extend the life, or increase the capability of the asset

impairment by catastrophe

sale for less than land value, if the asset is part of an operating business and is sold as a whole

OTHER VALUES

Values used for other purposes will change over time. For example, when an object is first acquired and put into service, its insurance value or replacement cost is the same as book value. However, after a period of time, these values will vary. Some items, such as vehicles, machinery, and computers, will probably decrease in market value, but may well increase in replacement cost. Buildings, on the other hand, will probably increase in both market value and replacement cost. Therefore, the value recorded for insurance purposes must be reviewed periodically, a new determination made, and records updated appropriately.

The procedures needed to determine other values are subject to interpretation. Most companies will periodically secure the services of an appraiser to establish these values. Insurance companies may provide advice and guidance to their customers. The services of appraisers, how to acquire them, and what they will do are covered in another book in the Wiley/Institute of Management Accountants (previously National Association of Accountants) Professional Book Series called *Corporate Valuation*. Please refer to that book for detailed information on the appraisal process.

It is important to recognize, though, that using wrong value procedures can lead to disaster for a business. Insurance rates are based on a percentage of the value at which the property is insured. Insurance values greater than replacement cost increase the premiums, but will not provide a greater return in case of destruction. On the other hand, insurance values below replacement cost will mean serious problems if the property is damaged or lost. Insurance companies pay the maximum of replacement cost or insured value, whichever is less. Most insurance policies pay replacement cost only if the insured value is greater than 80 percent of the replacement cost at the time of the casualty. When insured cost is less than 80 percent, the companies pay on replacement cost, less depreciation. The loss of buildings can be seen as the worst disaster, since the replacement cost is likely to have gone up in spite of the building's age and use.

Other types of problems with using the correct valuation for the purpose exist. For example, in a nonprofit trade association, the county tax assessor requested an inventory of business property for the purposes of establishing the personal property tax. The organization's bookkeeper had just received an insurance company assessment of replacement costs of its few assets. Because these are insured at replacement cost, that figure was much higher than current market value. This assessment was supplied to the tax assessor.

There was no property record, and the organization did not depreciate its equipment, in accordance with fund accounting principles. The tax assessor for a subsequent ten-year period did not request, nor did the association submit, revised equipment values. The assessment process was to add 5 percent per year to the original values it received in lieu of a new report. Therefore, the current tax assessment was based on a 50 percent increase on an originally inflated replacement cost.

In reality, the business property tax procedures call for market value of the property as the assessed value. The association still had most of the same property at the end of the ten-year period. Its market value was very low. Therefore, when correct reports were filed and reassessment occurred, the tax was reduced by 95 percent.

USES OF VALUES

Historical cost, or book value, is used to allocate costs to the periods used. It is accumulated as the purchase or invoice cost plus the cost to prepare the item for service. This cost is then depreciated over the periods of usefulness.

Other purposes are to establish the future value of an asset. That value will vary due to many different factors.

INSURANCE

Insurance valuation will be based upon the agreed upon actual cash or replacement value at the time the policy is issued. The premiums paid will be based on a percentage of that value. When a claim is made, that value normally represents the maximum that can be expected.

There are a number of problems involved in establishing that value and correcting it over the life of the item.

Construction costs are rising. That means that buildings and machinery will likely have a higher replacement cost. New technology may mean that replacement will not even occur on the same basis. Examples are construction techniques for older buildings made of brick or rock. These types of buildings, if damaged in an earthquake, may not be replaceable in the same style. Computer equipment more than a few years old may not be replaceable in like kind. Production line equipment, printing presses, and other machinery may dictate a number of different replacement possibilities.

Insurance policies can be written with many different types of coverage. This is not intended as an insurance analysis. However, the asset accountant should be aware of the replacement cost prior to establishing the insurance coverage. At the time of loss, it will be necessary to provide proof of loss. Property records that substantiate the existence and location are needed. Also, it is important to have recorded and maintained the record of the asset values. An assessment of deferred maintenance, as well as a record of maintenance expenditures on major items will support that proof of loss. This also points out the need for security and redundancy or backup for asset records. If a building is destroyed, the accounting records should be available at another location.

COLLATERAL FOR A LOAN

The price at which an asset can be sold to a willing buyer without undue pressure on either party is referred to as market, or fair market, value. When property is used as collateral for a loan, the lending institution will provide a loan at only a percentage of that value. If a foreclosure is necessary, the property must be sold quickly and probably in a distress sale. The carrying costs for the finance company can quickly reduce its value.

In considering options for financing, businesses must consider the resale values of their property. Financing can occur as specific mortgages on real estate and buildings. Also, banks or other financing sources may want a general mortgage on the property involved. Existence of a well-maintained and documented property record can enhance financing opportunities for both general credit lines, as well as those taking specific assets as collateral. Therefore, the collateral value is enhanced by good accounting and property record systems.

PURCHASE OR SALE OF A COMPLETE BUSINESS

In purchasing an operating business, the sales price is likely to be different from the book value of the property, plant, and equipment. Future sales value will enter into the price determination. When a price in excess of the book value is paid, that excess is recorded as goodwill on the purchasing company's books. However, if the purchase price is less than the book value, it is necessary to readjust the book value of property, plant, and equipment downward to reflect its purchase price. This is one of the few times that book value can be reduced on a still useable asset. Considerable discussion is currently occurring on the concept of accounting for impairments in fixed assets. There is not yet consensus as to the appropriateness of reductions based on an impairment in United States accounting practices.

FIRST CREATION OF PROPERTY RECORD

When called upon to create a property record for the first time, additional difficulties may be encountered. Many businesses have not maintained property records in the past. Such records have not been required of cities and other government agencies. Even where property records were established, many organizations have not accurately maintained them. Retirements and losses may not have been reflected in the record. Where location is a function of the property record, it may not be current. A significant task is required to create a property record for the first time in an operating business. Nearly as much effort is required to bring one up to date that has not been adequately maintained.

Review of the existing process establishing the proper property record and maintenance procedures is the first step. Then it will be necessary to do a physical review or inventory of the property remaining. Make an assessment of its current condition and if the original cost and date of purchase are not present in the property record, then it will be necessary to make an estimate of these items. From those figures, book costs can be established in a manner similar to that done when acquiring a new business.

VALUATION TECHNIQUES

Current market values are established by considering three methods.

(a) Present value of future cash flows—by making an assessment of the future in- and out-flows of cash, the net income for future period can be reduced to current value utilizing current value analysis.

(b) Comparable sales can be used to establish a second cost comparison figure. Where a current market exists for similar items, such as automobiles, airplanes, computers, and some production equipment, looking at recent comparable sales provides a good estimate of current market value. Real estate, land, and buildings are always appraised based on comparable sales. They must be within the same geographical area. Comparable real estate sales, even within the same town, may be considerably different if not in close proximity to one another.

(c) Historical cost, less deterioration, plus improvements (less costs to dispose of) is the third value determinant. Taking the original purchase price and reducing it based on observed wear and tear and obsolescence, then adding the improvements, provides a third bench mark for comparison of value purposes. Care must be taken that items that will have a negative value are also considered. Toxic chemical spills or presence of other negatives must be assessed as part of the depreciation. Also, the cost of disposition at some future date is appropriate to consider. For example, a nuclear energy plant or oil refinery may cost more for future decommissioning than the original cost.

Using these three measures of market value can provide the appraiser with sufficient information to arrive at an estimate of property value.

Land is always valued based on comparable sales. There is an established market for real estate and present value of current cash flows or historical costs less depreciation should not influence the appraisal value.

MANAGEMENT INFORMATION

Management must understand the various values to make correct decisions. Using the wrong value in making a decision can have serious consequences.

Return on investment is a required external analysis. The published financial reports are based on book value and that investment base is used for the analysis. However, for internal management purposes, it may be appropriate to use market values. When attempting to evaluate the effectiveness of an old plant with very low book value to a modern new plant with a high book value, there are problems. Return on investment using book value would indicate the older plant has a higher return. For internal management purposes, it may be appropriate to normalize in some fashion the value of the investments being compared. Using current market value of both, or simply recognizing that this comparison is invalid, is important to the management process.

The high rate of inflation has caused many incorrect management decisions in the past few years. Leveraged buyouts used to finance hostile takeovers have been one result. These have occurred in many cases because management was not aware of the actual market value of the component parts. Potential purchasers recognized that the market value of the individual components of a business were worth more than the current return on them. As a result, they purchased stock sufficient to take over the company and financed their purchase with debt secured by the inflated asset value of the firm. In many cases, they then liquidated the assets to reduce or eliminate the debt. Numerous businesses have been totally closed and sold off in pieces with the sale of individual assets bringing back significant profits to the purchaser.

Management must be aware of, and periodically consider, alternative uses of their assets. An old asset having substantial current market value may be a good candidate for sale and replacement with new technology. It may also be appropriate to discontinue a business line that is not providing an adequate return on the current market value. Either changing to a different product line or selling off the individual assets themselves to enter a new business line may be a better decision.

If management personnel has the information needed, they can make correct decisions. Knowing the various asset values will allow them to manage the assets for the best use. They can also make correct decisions and carry adequate insurance. Insurance premiums should not be greater than necessary for adequate coverage, however. Assessment of the state of deferred maintenance will allow the company to manage the asset as opposed to using it up. The manager responsible for the assets needs to know all of the values concerning that asset. Market value is just one.

PERIODIC ASSESSMENT OF VALUE

Because the values of property, plant, and equipment change over time, a periodic assessment of those values is necessary. This assessment can be done with a firm's own employees if they have the skills and time necessary to accomplish it. It can be done on a periodic basis, such as annually. Alternatively, it can be done when there is a change in responsible manager or departmental custodian. Normally, an assessment of deferred maintenance should be done whenever verification of the assets' existence occurs.

Assessment of other values is probably necessary about every five years. This depends on the rate of inflation and its impact on an individual company's property, plant, and equipment.

There are appraisal companies and consultants available to do all of these tasks. Contracting with an appraisal firm can bring an expert into the process.

There are many appraisal firms, either local or national. Also a number of public accounting and consulting firms providing this service. The selection of an outside appraisal firm is also an important decision. The recent savings and loan problems were caused in many cases by inflated appraisals on real estate and buildings. There has not been a requirement for appraisers to be certified. Effective January 1, 1992, the federal government has required certification of appraisers who assess the value of property financed or guaranteed by any federal program. These certification processes are being put into place by the various state governments. These certification processes vary from "grandfathering" those professionals who have been appraising for a number of years to individual testing of all candidates. It is appropriate, therefore, not to just accept the lowest offer for your appraisal contract, nor to assume that the certification of the appraisers is adequate to protect you. As a minimum, the firm must have adequate certified appraisers to accomplish the task.

In addition, look beyond the certification. For what other companies in your industry has the firm provided service? Are these certified appraisers members of professional societies? There are a number of professional societies and they have conflict of interest rules and codes of ethics to which their members voluntarily subscribe.

It is important to assure yourself that the appraisers assigned will have adequate specialization in your industry and type of equipment. Real estate appraisers may have no knowledge of your manufacturing process or the markets for your type of machinery.

Not reappraising periodically may be appropriate for your business. However, management should do an analysis and make a decision on a conscious basis. It is important for the asset accountant to periodically review a sample of assets in the current market. The asset accountant should be responsible for bringing to management's attention any discrepancies between insurance values, replacement costs, and current market values of their assets.

8

ALLOCATION OF COSTS TO ACCOUNTING PERIODS

INTRODUCTION

As described in preceding chapters, property, plant, and equipment that lasts for more than one year are charged to capital accounts. It is necessary to recognize the appropriate portion of that cost of using up property, plant, and equipment in each succeeding accounting period. The matching principle of accounting requires expenses to be recognized during the period that they generate revenue during the normal business cycle. In addition, cost reimbursement systems must include the using up of the property, plant, and equipment. In setting prices for products and services, management must consider all costs incurred. Unless a portion of the costs of property, plant, and equipment purchased in prior years is included, prices might be set too low. Likewise, cost of property, plant, and equipment purchased in the current year, but used for a number of years in the future, should not all be included in setting today's minimum price levels.

Generally accepted accounting principles provide the rules for financial reporting. In addition to the financial requirements, management must have information to allow them to make reasonable decisions regarding new products, product continuation, and budgeting for replacement of capital assets.

COSTS OF USING UP ASSETS

The accounting rules for recognizing the cost of assets is sometimes confused with providing sufficient dollars to replace them. The depreciation or the recognition of the declining usefulness of assets has nothing to do with its financing. This is descriptively outlined in GAAP. (*ARB 43* chapter 9, section C, paragraph 5)

> The cost of a productive facility is one of the costs of the services it renders during its useful economic life. GAAP requires that the cost be spread over the expected useful life of the facility in such a way as to allocate it as equitably as possible to the periods during which services are obtained from the use of the facility. This procedure is known as depreciation accounting, a system of accounting which aims to distribute the cost or other basic value of tangible capital assets, less salvage (if any) of the estimated useful life of the unit (which may be a group of assets) in a systematic and rational matter. It is a process of allocation, not valuation.

The Financial Accounting Standards Board in *Concept Statement 5 Par. 8bc* describes the consumption of benefits: "Some expenses, such as depreciation . . . are allocated by systematic and rational procedures to the periods during which the related assets are expected to provide benefits." *Concept Statement 6* defines assets, accrual accounting, and the concept of depreciation. Because several periods may elapse between the time cash is invested in property, plant, and equipment, and the time products are produced, accrual accounting is used. The purpose of accrual accounting is the allocation or deferral of revenues, expenses, gains, and losses to the appropriate period to reflect an entity's performance during that period instead of just listing its cash receipts and outlays.

Accrual accounting is to reflect in the current accounting period those expenses which are applicable to the activities of that period. FASB Concept Statement VI, Paragraph 145 states the goal of accrual accounting.

> The goal of accrual accounting is to account in the periods in which they occur for the effects on an entity of transactions and other events and circumstances, to the extent that those financial effects are recognizable and measurable.

As described in Chapter 2, "What Is an Asset?", assets including property, plant, and equipment are probable future economic benefits obtained or controlled by the entity of a result of past transactions. Once acquired, it continues to be an asset until the organization collects it, transfers it, or uses it up. The process of recognizing the use and deterioration of property, plant, and equipment is called depreciation.

DEPRECIATION

Depreciation is "the process of allocating costs of tangible assets over periods benefitted (expected life of asset). It represents the gradual exhaustion of the service capacity of fixed assets through periodic charges to obsolescent action to operations. It is the consequence of such factors as use, obsolescence, inadequacy, and wear." (*IMA Statement Number 2A*) In measuring the amount of depreciation to recognize in a specific period there are three variables:

Estimated life

Cost, less estimated salvage value

Allocation method

ESTIMATED LIFE

It is necessary to determine the estimated life of each piece of property, plant, and equipment as it will be used in the entity involved. However, as a matter of expediency, most organizations establish classes or groups of items and depreciate them over a similar life. For example, furniture may be defined as a class and a single life utilized for it. Because it is necessary to project into the future, this is not a simple task. Useful lives of items may be far beyond what the practical or economic life of an item will be.

Automobiles may have a useful life of ten or twelve years. However, or in a rental car business, the practice may be to replace an automobile each year, or within two years. Because customers expect to drive new automobiles, the economic life in the rental car business would be no more than two years. The same automobiles used by administrative employees of the rental company may be replaced every three or four years. Past practice should be reviewed in determining the future useful life of the item.

Determining the estimated useful life has a significant impact on the period expenses. Shortening the life will increase expenses in the periods. An estimated life in excess of actual life understates the expenses in those periods and will cause retirement of undepreciated assets. Therefore, careful consideration should be given to ensuring that estimated life and actuals are reasonably accurate.

The use of property record retirement information can be of assistance. Known as mortality or vintage records, the past lives of assets and classes of assets can be of assistance. It may not predict the future, however, it may serve as a possible indicator. Examples are computers and aircraft. Although the possible useful life may be ten years, the technology is increasing so rapidly, that it is not unusual for a computer to be replaced in two or three years. Aircraft purchased by major airlines in the past were normally replaced as new models came out. The major airlines sold the aircraft to smaller airlines who continued to operate them for a number of years. In recent years however, new models of aircraft have not been produced as often. Therefore, aircraft have been left on line for twenty to twenty-five years by major air carriers. Now the cost of maintenance of those aircraft is becoming the motivating factor for replacement.

In determining the estimated life, consider the lives of similar items used by the company in the past. A well-defined property record will provide that type of information. Review with the users of the items their expected use in the future. Is it increasing or decreasing? Determine what policies may be changed that will affect the actual life of an item in the organization.

Many small businesses tend to use the lives authorized in the internal revenue regulations for income tax. If these lives are close to what the estimated ones are, that may be a reasonable thing to do. However, tax regulations are produced to implement social and economic programs and carry out these government policies. Examples are accelerated depreciation allowing large deductions and therefore lower taxes in the early life of assets. This tax policy may stimulate your organization to replace items quickly and may artificially shorten the life. However, if the actual use in the company is longer than the tax life, using tax life will substantially affect expenses per period and the net asset book values.

COST BASIS

The allocation base used is historical cost as established in the property record, less estimated salvage value. Salvage value will be the amount that can be recovered, less cost of removing the item. Salvage value may range from nothing for electronic equipment or machinery that will be disposed of in a landfill, to a considerable amount in the case of a rental car sold after only two years. Salvage value can be negative, however, as in the case of a nuclear power plant, which may cost more to dismantle and remove from service than the original construction costs. Establishing historical book cost was outlined in Chapter 7, "Establishing Value."

ALLOCATION METHODS

Straight Line Depreciation

This method of determining depreciation expense only uses a time variable. It is computed by dividing the asset base by the number of years of estimated life:

$$\text{depreciation expense} = \frac{\text{historical cost}}{\text{estimated life in years}}$$

This is the simplest method and, where the usefulness of the asset is equal over its entire life, is an appropriate method. Other methods take into consideration uses that are not equal or linear over the life of the asset.

Units of Production

A number of equipment and plant items deteriorate by use rather than with time. Aircraft engines, tractors, and construction equipment can have a measured life in hours of use. Trucks, vehicles, and other rolling equipment may be measured by number of miles before replacement is appropriate. In this method, depreciation expense is determined by multiplying the historical cost by a percentage of estimated life in hours, divided by hours of use in a period.

Using the units of production depreciation method would be important on production lines that may be used only one shift some years, and up to three shifts in others. Depreciation practices should recognize these different uses in determining depreciation expense for the period. Similarly, airlines that use an aircraft for significant hours during one period and place it in storage when business is not so great can recognize that difference by using this depreciation method.

ACCELERATED DEPRECIATION

Accelerated methods of depreciation are primarily tax methods. By accelerating the depreciation in the early periods and allowing reduced taxes during that time, the government provides an incentive for business to purchase new plant and equipment. However, there are rationales for accelerating depreciation in estimating the book depreciation also.

Low Maintenance Cost in Early Accounting Periods

Where equipment has low maintenance costs when it is new and greater costs as the equipment ages, a flatter expense over the life of the equipment will be recognized through accelerated depreciation. Depreciation expense is accelerated in the early years when maintenance expense is low, and reduces in later years when maintenance expenses have increased. The typical methods for accelerating depreciation are:

Sum of years digits

Declining balance

Double or 150 percent depreciation

Sum of Years Digits

This method results in a decreasing charge as a result of a decreasing fraction of the years of remaining life over the sum of the total years.

In this method, a sum of the total years is determined, for example, a five-year life would be (5 + 4 + 3 + 2 + 1 = 15). This figure is constant over the five-year life. The first year there are five remaining years, therefore depreciation will be 5/15. For the second year depreciation will be 4/15, etc. (5/15, 4/15, 3/15, 2/15, and 1/15). There will thus be five times as much depreciation in the first year as in the last.

Declining Balance Methods

The declining balance produces a decreasing depreciation expense by expressing a depreciation rate that is some multiple of the straight-line method rate. An item with an estimated ten-year life has a straight-line rate of 10 percent per year. A double declining balance rate would be 20 percent per year multiplied by the remaining book value.

Year	Rate	Remaining Base	Year's Depreciation
1	20%	10,000	3,000
2	20%	8,000	1,600
3	20%	6,400	1,280
4	20%	5,120	1,024
5	20%	4,096	819

When the declining rate goes below what would have occurred on a straight-line basis, there is generally a conversion to straight line for the remaining life.

The most typical of the declining balance methods are double declining, or 150 percent declining balance methods.

OTHER DEPRECIATION CONCERNS

Use Beyond Expected Life

Depreciation is the process of allocating book cost over the accounting periods of the assets used. However, if the asset is continued in use beyond the estimated life, it will have been fully depreciated. Once the book cost (less applicable salvage) has been expensed, no further depreciation is appropriate.

This condition may be the result of an incorrect original estimate of useful life, or the conditions may have changed. During periods of economic stress, a car rental agency may change its policy and continue to use cars for another year before replacement. The year such a policy is placed in effect depreciation expenses will be significantly reduced and net profits will increase. It is appropriate to make management aware of this impact and to review the estimated life of remaining assets. Where conditions or policies have changed, it is appropriate to consider and change the estimated remaining life of assets that have not been fully depreciated. For management information purposes, it may be appropriate to restate historical periods and show what depreciation would be in the current period, had the life been estimated accurately in the beginning. However, generally accepted accounting principles do not allow such a change on the published financial statements.

Physical Deterioration

Depreciation is based on an accounting theory of spreading costs over periods of usefulness. It does not as a normal function consider actual physical deterioration. Where maintenance has been neglected, or where other natural phenomenon caused significant deterioration, it should be reviewed and recognized. A piece of construction equipment left out in the weather, even though not used, may deteriorate significantly. Similarly, lack of paint to seal a building from the elements may cause significant deterioration early in its useful life. It is important to review assets and determine a plan of approach of maintenance to bring them back to full future use. The alternative is to recognize the reduced value, write down the equipment value, and take the expense in the current period.

Functional Obsolescence

New technology may be developed and produced requiring reconsideration of the useful life of existing assets. Production machinery that is faster and produces better quality at a lower cost may make the production line obsolete overnight. Computers that have capabilities of running new software that will provide additional services may require replacement earlier than anticipated. When a policy decision is made to retire and replace plant and equipment earlier than its estimated life, depreciation lives should be reconsidered and adjusted accordingly.

Economical Obsolescence

High maintenance costs may require replacement earlier than anticipated. There may be a better alternative, such as selling aircraft for a greater total return, which is more cost effective than continuing to operate them. A review of market value versus rate of return on production of assets is appropriate periodically. Where the current market value of equipment is greater than the combined future return on production, sale of the asset is a better alternative.

TAX VS. BOOK DEPRECIATION

Many small businesses use the same depreciation methods for both financial statements and tax purposes. Where the benefit to management does not justify the additional cost of multiple depreciation methods, this would be appropriate. However, it must be recognized that the tax system is social policy, not generally acceptable accounting principles. Using tax depreciation methods in many cases will give the wrong signals to management. The high expenses allocated to products or methods could cause a decision to discontinue those products or services.

BALANCE SHEET DISCLOSURE

Generally accepted accounting principals require disclosure on a balance sheet of total depreciation expense for the period, balances of major classes of depreciable assets, and accumulating depreciation, either by major class of asset or in total. In addition, a general description of the method or methods used in computing depreciation must be outlined for major classes of depreciable assets. These disclosures should be readily available from a well-designed property record system.

NOT-FOR-PROFIT ORGANIZATIONS

Because not-for-profit organizations do not exist for the purpose of generating a profit, and in fact many do not have revenue streams from services, they have not historically recognized depreciation expense. However, the management of assets is even stronger in not-for-profit organizations than in profit-making organizations. Members of the board of directors and senior management of nonprofit organizations have a higher responsibility to stewardship of assets than to boards and management of publicly held corporations. The Financial Accounting Standards Board in issuing Statement 93 established that "not-for-profit organizations shall recognize the cost of using up the future economic benefits or service potentials of their long lived tangible assets—depreciation—and shall disclose the following . . . requirements are the same as APB 12 for other businesses. . . ." Therefore, generally accepted accounting principles require financial statements of not-for-profit organizations to compute and disclose depreciation.

GOVERNMENT ACCOUNTING FOR DEPRECIATION

Generally accepted accounting principles for government is currently in a period of flux. The Government Accounting Standards Board has not yet ruled on the issue. It has a major project underway to investigate and determine the appropriate accounting for general fixed assets and recording depreciation on them. However, enterprise government organizations, which operate in the same fashion as businesses, are required to use depreciation accounting.

Government accounting distinguishes between general fixed assets such as infrastructure, roads, sidewalks, sewer systems, etc. and other assets. Depreciation of general fixed assets are not recorded current. Generally accepted accounting practices for government does not allow depreciation of general fixed assets to be recorded in the accounts of government funds. It may be included in cost accounting systems for cost analysis and may be recorded in the separate general fixed assets account group (GFAAG). The general fixed assets account group is a separate accounting fund. In government accounting, a fund is the same as setting up a separate company or reporting entity.

Depreciation is an element of expense resulting from the use of long-lived assets. It is conveniently measured by allocating the expected net cost of using the asset over the estimated useful life in a systematic and rational manner. The discussions on government GAAP and the recommendation that depreciation not be recorded in the governmental fund accounts neither denies its existence nor precludes calculating depreciation to determine total and/or unit costs.

SFAB 93 requires that depreciation be recognized on enterprise accounting functions. Enterprise accounts are those that operate similar to a business and collect revenues or user fees. Examples are airports, sewer systems, transit systems, etc. The Government Accounting Standards Board has stated that colleges, universities, and other governmental entities considered by the Financial Accounting Standards Board to not be not-for-profit organizations should not change their accounting to include depreciation. The GASB is considering depreciation and other fixed asset questions in a number of proceedings.

Until these questions are resolved, GAAP for government is in question. None of the arguments about not recording governmental depreciation exclude it from the cost-based fee setting or the management of assets. Most argue that because governments and not-for-profit organizations are not in business to make a profit, but rather to provide services, depreciation is not a cost to the entity. Where there is no profit to be calculated, the logic is that depreciation is not appropriate.

This is not a valid position because depreciation is recognition of the cost of using up the asset. Unless the cost is included, assets cannot be managed. All of the infrastructure that our government put in place is being used up, or has been used, with no consideration for replacement. Put it in place, use it, but don't manage it has been the prevailing attitude. Planning for replacement has only occurred after it was obvious the asset had been used up.

In the past, lack of planning has worked. A bond issue or other financing mechanism was used to replace used up government infrastructure.

Capital financing limits are currently being approached and a great number of infrastructure assets are all wearing out at the same time. Accounting must change to provide information to government managers so they can plan and meet the needs of tomorrow.

There is really little difference between the needs of government, not-for-profit, and business managers.

Most of the arguments for similar GAAP for government, not-for-profit organizations, and businesses are coming from those who must use the financial statements to measure government's performance. Accountants providing services to watchdog groups such as the General Accounting Office and other audit groups are demanding information allowing for the same management of assets as occurs in business. Another book in the John Wiley series, *Financial and Auditing Guide for Not-For-Profit Organizations*, Malvern J. Gross, Jr., William Warshauer, Jr., and Richard F. Larkin goes into considerable detail in this accounting and may be referred to for more detailed information on not-for-profit accounting. The authors offer a good argument for recording depreciation:

> Depreciation accounting is now required for most not-for-profit organizations that want to describe their financial statements as being in conformity with generally accepted accounting principles. Aside from these requirements, the authors believe that depreciation accounting is desirable for most not-for-profit organizations for a number of reasons.
>
> Most not-for-profit organizations provide services that are measured in terms of costs. Depreciation is a cost. By not including this cost, the reader is misled into thinking that the actual costs were less than they really were. The board in an organization is charged with the responsibility of efficiently using all of the resources available to it to carry out the program of the organization. By excluding a significant amount from the cost of the program, the board gives the reader the impression that the program has been carried out more efficiently than is actually the case. *Financial and Auditing Guide for Not-for-Profit Organizations*, Fourth Edition

The same arguments can be aimed at government accounting. Government charges utility companies that dig up their roads for the cost of repairing the damage. The cost of laying pavement by a road department cannot be determined unless depreciation is included in the calculation. More and more government services are being offered on a fee basis. Government managers have no way of knowing if the fees charged actually reimburse the costs incurred without including depreciation on general fixed assets in the calculation. Therefore, it is believed that in the future, government GAAP will also require depreciation to be recognized and reported.

9

REGULATED UTILITIES

INTRODUCTION

Most businesses have a number of external reporting requirements. These differing requirements affect the manner in which property records must be maintained. Other chapters discussed the generally accepted accounting principles required on securities and exchange commission financial statements and the federal and state income tax information that must be kept.

Regulated utilities must also consider the requirements of the regulatory body when designing property accounting systems. They must meet all the requirements that other businesses do and in addition give consideration to the regulatory requirements. Most regulated industries have only one regulator but the telephone industry must meet the requirements of both the Federal Communications Commission and State Public Utility Commissions.

Although accountants establishing records in non-regulated industries need not concern themselves with the regulatory requirements, this chapter may be of benefit by suggesting solutions to accounting problems that are also applicable to them. The Federal Communications Commission and the Interstate Commerce Commission have established detailed accounting requirements for the companies they regulate. This chapter will briefly describe some of those requirements. Also, the references to the Code of Federal Regulations, where they are spelled out in detail, is provided. Accountants in regulated industries should refer to those regulations for direction. Accountants in non-regulated industries may find the regulations useful.

DIFFERENCES IN GAAP

The Financial Accounting Standards Board in its Statement 71 considered what impact rate-making and regulatory bodies have on regulated utilities. They concluded that regulated utilities should not just follow regulated prescribed accounting where it differed from generally accepted accounting principles. However, the Board acknowledged that regulation does have an impact on regulated companies. They concluded that "rate regulation should be considered."

The net impact of SFAS 71 is to establish that if rates are set by regulatory bodies based on the actual costs of the regulated utility, and there is reasonable assurance that market factors will allow those rates to be collected, then the regulatory prescribed accounting for determining costs should be followed. An example of that is the allowance by the Interstate Commerce Commission of a $5,000 minimum threshold for capitalizing assets. They provide that railroads should expense any item other than land and track costing less than $5,000. In contrast, the Federal Communications Commission provides a threshold of $200 in determining capital and expense for most of the accounts.

The cost included in establishing asset value can be based on what the regulatory body specifies in its detailed accounting system if that regulatory body has rate-making ability and can provide assurance that future rates will include the cost of recovery of that capital as well as a rate of return on it.

Most regulatory bodies specify the detailed accounting that the companies they regulate must use. That includes a chart of accounts and the definitions and description of a detailed property record.

During the 1980s a push for federal deregulation has entirely eliminated regulation of the airlines by the Civil Aeronautics Board and of the trucking industry by the Interstate Commerce Commission. Deregulation is also changing the telecommunications and railroad industries.

TELECOMMUNICATIONS ACCOUNTING

The Federal Communications Commission (FCC) was authorized in 1933 to provide detailed regulation of the telephone industry.

Prior to that, the telephone industry had been regulated by the Interstate Commerce Commission (ICC) commencing in 1912. The details of the FCC regulation is spelled out in the *Code of Federal Regulations* (CFR) Title 47, Part 32. That Part was issued in 1986 and basically adhered to generally accepted accounting principals at that time.

Telecommunications plant is defined as that which ordinarily has a life of more than one year and a value greater than $200. It is maintained at original cost.

An exception to original cost is telecommunications plant purchased in service. Where either an entire company or part of one has been purchased, the purchasing company must place the asset in the regulated books of account at the original cost paid by the original company. Any accrued appreciation that has been allowed through rates must be incorporated within the accumulated depreciation accounts. Any amount paid for the operating plant in addition to its original cost is included in an account 2005—telecommunications plant adjustment. This account is either written off over a reasonable period to a non-operating account, which is not provided for in authorized rates or, under special circumstances, the Federal Communications Commission may authorize its recovery. The regulatory concept here is that the rate payers should only be required to pay for the original cost of putting it into telephone service. Any increase in market value should accrue to the late payers and not the telecommunications company.

BASIC PROPERTY RECORD

There is a requirement that all telephone companies maintain a basic property record. It is defined as that portion of the total property accounting system that preserves the following detailed information:

The identity, vintage, location, and original cost of units of property

Original ongoing transaction data in terms of such units

Any specific financial and cost accounting information not requiring separate disclosure as an account, but which is needed to support regulatory, cost, tax, management and other specific accounting information needs and requirements

Further, basic property records must be:

Subject to internal auditing controls

Auditable

Equal in the aggregate to the total investment in the general ledger account

Equal in the aggregate to the total cost allocations supporting the determination of cost of service. The record must maintain cost of service data for a particular point in time and maintain throughout the life of the property

Each company is required to file with the FCC a copy of a complete plan of the method used in the compilation of a basic property record. The plan must include a list of property record units to be used under each regulated plant account. The continuing property record must be compiled on the basis of original cost or other book cost that is consistent with the required system of accounts. It is required to be maintained in a manner that will meet a number of basic objectives. It must:

Provide for the verification of property record units by physical examination

Provide for accurate accounting for retirements

Provide data for use in conjunction with depreciation studies

Further, the design of the property record is required to provide the description, location, date of placement, essential details of construction, and original cost of each of the property record units. Much of the telecommunications plant is constructed by the company and it further requires that underlying records of construction cost be maintained, so that upon retirement of one or more retirement units the actual cost, or a reasonable estimate of the plant retired, can be determined. Costs must be maintained by specific location for property record units contained in certain accounts. These are land, buildings, telephone equipment, motor vehicles, garages, and furniture.

Average costs are allowed to be developed for plant, which consists of a large number of similar items. In telecommunications activities, poles, wire, cable, cable terminals, conduit, furniture, and work equipment are allowed to be averaged. However, those average costs must be included in a vintage or band of years, and average costs must be determined for those years within an accounting area. The establishment of an accounting area is left to the companies: it must be a geographic area in which accounting records for all general ledger asset accounts are maintained. The only other requirement is that it not cross state lines or other regulatory boundaries.

Basic property or retirement units are distinguished from minor items. Whereas the units must be maintained in detail in the property record, minor items do not. Minor items are those that are less than a base unit; they are included in the cost of a retirement or property unit. No accounting is necessary when a minor item is retired. Cost of replacement is charged to the applicable repair account for the property.

Replacement of minor items that effect a substantial betterment, and make the property more useful, of greater durability, or of greater capacity, requires that the excess cost of this replacement over the estimate of the one retired be included in the cost of the property record item. The chart of accounts required for telecommunications plant is as follows.

REGULATED PLANT

Property, plant, and equipment:

Telecommunications plant and service	2001
Property held for future telecommunications use	2002
Plant under construction, short term	2003
Plant under construction, long term	2004
Plant acquired adjustment	2005
Nonoperating plant	2006
Goodwill	2007

TELECOMMUNICATIONS PLANT IN SERVICE
CHART OF ACCOUNTS

The detailed chart of accounts for telecommunications companies is outlined by the Federal Communications Commission as follows:

General support assets

Land	2111
Motor vehicles	2112
Aircraft	2113
Special purpose vehicles	2114
Garage work equipment	2115
Other work equipment	2116
Buildings	2121
Furniture	2122
Office equipment	2123
General purpose computers	2124
Analog electronic switching	2211
Digital electronic switching	2212
Electro-mechanical switching	2215
Operator systems	2220
Radio systems	2231
Circuit equipment	2232
Station apparatus	2311
Customer premises wiring	2321
Large private branch exchanges	2341
Public telephone equipment	2351
Other terminal equipment	2361
Poles	2411
Aerial cable	2421
Underground cable	2422
Buried cable	2423
Submarine cable	2424

RAILROADS

The Interstate Commerce Commission outlines a detailed accounting process for railroad companies. It is published in the *Code of*

Federal Regulations, Title 49, Part 1200. The ICC Uniform System of Accounts for Railroads was originally developed in 1907. That system of accounting did not include depreciation, but was based on betterment accounting concepts. The Railroad Revitalization and Regulatory Reform Act of 1976 was enacted by Congress to improve the financial viability of the nation's railroads. Among other things, it emphasized the need for the ICC to use more accurate accounting and costs data. In response to that need, the ICC created the new Uniform System of Accounts in 1987. The ICC also began a program to replace its existing costing system with a more sophisticated uniform rail costing system (URCS). Congress continued to emphasize the changes needed in railroad accounting by creating a Railroad Accounting Principles Board in 1980 with the responsibilities to: 1) establish a body of cost accounting principles and 2) to make administrative and legislative recommendations as it deems necessary to integrate the principles into the regulatory process. The Railroad Accounting Principles Board created a final report in 1987 which explores a number of principles of asset accounting. They expound a statement of principle.

> Assets shall be valued at either the value of the resource forgone by the entity to acquire the assets (GAP costs) or at the current market value, depending on the regulatory applications. The method of valuing assets in each application shall be determined by the causality principle:

The Board concluded that no single asset valuation method is appropriate for all regulatory applications. A number of problems are discussed in this final report. Anyone interested in the concept of historical cost versus current market value for valuing assets, will find this report a valuable resource.

However, the result is that the common GAAP historical cost method is the appropriate one for allocating the cost of assets over future accounting periods.

RAILROAD USOA

Railroad carriers may prepare and publish financial statements to stockholders and others based on generally accepted accounting principles. However, any variance from the ICC's prescribed accounting rules that are contained in such statements must be clearly disclosed in its footnotes. Financial reports submitted as required to the ICC must be based on the Commission's prescribed accounting rules.

As new FASB standards are issued, the ICC bureau of accounts will review and issue an accounting series circular specifying whether or not the new standard is to be used in reports to the Commission. In addition to the accounting policies presented in the ICC regulations, all disclosures relating to APB opinions and FASB statements adopted by the Commission are required.

PROPERTY ACCOUNTS

The cost of purchase, construction, and betterment of property must be charged to the appropriate property account. Cost is defined as the cash disbursed or other fair value of assets distributed or the present value of amounts to be paid.

There is, however, an exception for a minimum capitalization rule:

> "When the cost of acquisition of units of road property and of additions to existing units of road property is less than $5,000, such costs may be charged to operating expenses." (Code of Federal Regulations 49 CFR Part 1201 p 25.)

COST OF CONSTRUCTION

A detailed description of what may be included in components of construction cost is outlined in the regulations.

Cost of Labor

This is defined to include labor and all associated fringe benefits such as vacation and holiday pay, health and welfare group insurance, pensions, and retirements plans, payroll taxes, and unemployment insurance. Also, any other personal expenses of employees when borne by the carrier, as well as the cost of fidelity bonds and employer's liability insurance premiums.

Officers or employees who are especially assigned to construction work charge their traveling and incidental expenses while engaged. However, there is a distinction between those especially assigned and one who merely renders service incidentally in connection with their work, such as general officers and employees. The latter shall not be charged to construction.

Cost of Materials and Supplies

This includes the purchase price of materials and supplies, including small tools, as well as the cost of inspection and loading assumed by the carrier. Similarly, a portion of store expenses, as well as taxes, are charged to the cost of construction.

Cost of Work Train Service

This includes amounts paid to others for rent and maintenance of equipment, as well as cost of labor or engine crews used in construction and crews held in readiness for such service.

Cost of Special Machine Service

This includes the cost of labor expended and of materials and supplies consumed in maintaining and operating power shovels, scrapers, rail unloaders, ballast unloaders, pile drivers, dredges, and other labor-saving machines. Also included are rents paid for the use of such machinery.

Cost of Transportation

This includes amounts paid to other companies for transportation of workers, materials, and supplies in connection with construction projects.

Cost of Contract Work

This includes amounts paid for work performed under contract by other companies, as well as any costs incidental to the award of the contract.

Cost of Protection from Casualty

This includes costs for protection against fire, such as firefighting or smoke detection equipment. Also included are payments to municipalities for fire protection during construction.

Cost of Injuries and Damages

This includes costs of injuries to people or property incurred directly as a result of construction projects. It also includes premiums paid for insurance applicable to the period prior to the completion of a construction project. It includes the cost of insurance to cover the construction amount. The receipts from insurance coverage for damage to property incidental to construction shall be credited to the accounts chartable for the expenditures necessary for restoring the damaged property.

Cost of Privileges

This includes the cost for temporary privileges defined as use of public property or streets in conjunction with railroad construction.

Material Excavated

This is the cost of disposing of material as well as removing and dumping.

Interest Cost

This is the cost of interest actually incurred. This is the cost of debt necessary to provide financing during the construction period, which includes the time required to get the asset ready for its intended use.

UNITS OF PROPERTY

Units of property that must be maintained in detail are listed in the regulations. By account, they are classified as depreciable.

Minor items that are components of a larger unit, when replaced, are treated as maintenance and charged to operating expenses. It should also be noted that the minimum rule of $5,000 applicable to charging cost of acquisition of units does not eliminate the requirement for removing the original cost of the unit from the account when the property is retired.

When a unit of property is retired, with or without replacement, the cost thereof shall be written out of the property account at the time of retirement. Its service value is charged to account seven hundred and thirty-five, accumulated depreciation. In order for the carrier to comply with these requirements, a detailed property record must be maintained. It is left to the carrier to design and implement such a record.

LIST OF UNITS OF PROPERTY

The regulations establish a list for the purpose of designating the units of property to be used in accounting for additions and retirements of property. This list is quite definitive and outlined by account. A few examples follow:

Account 3, grading

A retaining wall, rip wrap, hand placed, a protecting dike, a protecting crib, a wing jam, a revetment, mattress, pipe, or other structures to provide drainage. Each entire installation

Account 5, tunnels and subways

The entire masonry, entire timber, and entire metal lining of a tunnel or subway, including portals and wing walls

Drainage, entire installation
Lighting, each entire installation
Ventilation, each entire installation

Account 6, bridges, trestles, and culverts

A steel superstructure

A concrete or stone substructure

A concrete trestle, a complete bridge or approach

A timber trestle, a complete bridge or approach

Complete machinery for operating a movable span

A protecting dike, a protecting crib (a fencer), a wing dam, a complete culvert

Each entire installation

Account 20, shops and engine houses

A complete building, including attached platform

A complete platform structurally detached from a building

A turntable

A turntable pit

A transfer table with machinery

A transfer table pit

A sand storage and handling and drying apparatus

Outdoor binds, each complete installation

A lorry track system, (outside)

A boiler washing plant, each complete installation

An overhead crane outside

Each outside pipe installation, steam, air, water, etc.

Each sewer installation, storm or sanitary

Paving each complete installation

Each shop fence or wall installation

Any applicable unit

Account 58 miscellaneous equipment

An airplane

A complete vehicle

Account 59, computer systems and word processing equipment

A mainframe

A mini-computer

A word processing system

A printer

A monitor

A modem

A storage device

ACCOUNTING FOR ENGINEERING COSTS

The regulations require the pay and expenses of certain engineers, assistants, and clerks involved in survey and construction to be included in the cost of the particular property involved. Here is a list of officers and employees who must be involved:

Chief engineer

Assistant engineer

Bridge and signal engineer

Architects and draftsmen

Chief clerk and other clerks

Transit men and level men

Rod men and chain men

Cooks and porters on business cars

Following is a list of items of expense in conjunction with engineering:

Atlas and maps

Barometers

Books for office use

Business car service

Cameras

Compasses

Camp equipage

Chains for surveyors

Drawing boards

Drawing equipment

Field glasses

Furniture repairs and renewals

Heating and lighting

Magnets and magnifiers

Official train service

Paper, blueprint

Periodicals and newspapers

Photographic supplies

Printing and stationary

Provisions for business cars

Rent and repairs of offices

Rods for surveyors

Sextans and slide rules

Telegraph and telephone service

Traveling expenses

Triangles and tripods

COMMON AND CONTRACT MOTOR CARRIERS OF PASSENGERS

As part of the deregulation of motor carriers, the uniform system of accounts for motor carriers is no longer prescribed by the ICC. Motor carriers may follow GAAP for all accounting and reporting matters. However, the uniform system of accounts has been left in place for reference purposes, and is the basis for motor carrier reporting. Detailed report requirements are outlined in Parts 1240–1259 of the regulations.

CARRIER OPERATING PROPERTY

Carrier operating property is defined as property that is used actually and necessarily in current service or is ready and reasonably required for future service. It must have an expected life in service of more than one year from the date of installation. The cost of operating property is to be reported as part of a specified property accounts.

The cost is to be maintained in records that allow the determination of depreciation expenses over its life.

DEPRECIATION

Depreciation is to be applied on either a straight-line or mileage method (for automobile equipment). The regulations have defined depreciation as meaning the loss of service value not restored by current maintenance incurred in connection with the consumption or prospective retirement of the property in the course of service. Among the causes to be given consideration in determining depreciation lives, are wear and tear, decay, action of the elements, obsolescence, changes in the art, inadequacy, changes in demand, and requirements of public authority.

Depreciation for some accounts is accomplished on a unit plan basis. The unit plan requires that detailed property records be maintained that provide for the determination of the original historical costs of each individual unit upon retirement.

Some accounts allow for a group depreciation plan. Under a group plan, depreciation charges are accrued on the basis of a sum total of book cost balances. Rates are determined based on the average service life of the property within the account. On retirement of units of this property, the full service value is charged to the depreciation reserve without regard to whether the particular item has obtained the average service life. However, when a unit of property under the group plan is retired from service, the book cost of that unit is to be credited to the appropriate property account. Therefore, some means of determining the vintage of the property unit must be available.

MINOR ITEMS

A minor item is defined as one that is part of a unit of property.

Units of property are not defined in the USOA, but each carrier must submit a list of the property units upon which their records are maintained. Further, reporting requirements within the regulations do require determination of property units. The definition of a number of the accounts identify the property units.

UNIFORM SYSTEM OF ACCOUNTS— TANGIBLE ACCOUNTS

The various operating property accounts are maintained at original cost for all property normally having a service life of more than one year. Records are kept so as to separately reflect the cost and date of acquisition of each structure or unit of equipment. At the option of the carrier, each body, chassis, or other major part may be designated as separate property units. Details must appear in supporting records showing the cost of removal, cost of replacement, dates of activity, whether it is used or new equipment, and any increase in its capacity.

ACCOUNT DEFINITIONS

1201   Land and Land Rights

This account includes the cost of land or interest in land having a life of more than one year for use directly in connection with the motor carrier operations of the carrier for such purposes as general office, buildings, shops, garages, stations, terminals, waiting rooms, shelters, loading platforms, warehouses, and the like. It also includes the cost of buildings and other improvements constructed on the property.

The records must be maintained so as to show separately the cost of each parcel of land and the purpose or purposes for which it is used in carrier operations. Items of costs are identified as:

Clearing land of brush, trees, and debris (first cost of)

Condemnation proceedings, including court costs and special counsel fees

Consensus and abutting damages, payment for

Conveyances and notary fees

Easements and rights of way, cost of, and expenses of acquisition

Fees and commissions to brokers and agents

Grading

Land, cost of

Relocation property of others

Rights of way, including costs of locating

Sidewalks on public streets, abutting carrier's property

Special assessments on the basis of benefits for new roads, etc.

Surveys

Taxes assumed, acquired prior to the date of transfer of title

1211   Structure

This account includes the cost of structures used in motor carrier operations. This includes building or constructions to house, support, or safeguard property or persons, with all appurtenant fixtures permanently attached hereto and improvements to land or other structures, or constructions.

Records must show separately the cost of each structure included in the account and the purposes for which it is used in motor carrier operations. Items to be included are:

Architects' plans

Ash pits

Awnings

Boilers, furnaces, piping, wiring, fixtures and machinery for heating, lighting signaling, ventilating, and plumbing

Bridges and culverts

Chimneys

Commissions and fees to brokers, agents, architects, and others

Conduits (not to be removed)

Damages to abutting property during construction

Drainage and sewerage systems

Elevators, cranes, hoists, etc. and the machinery for operating them

Excavation, including shoring bracing, bridging, fill and disposal of excess material

Fences and hedges

Fire protection systems

Floor covering (permanently attached)

Foundations and piers

Grading and preparing grounds for buildings, including landscaping of grounds after construction

Outside lighting systems

Painting, first

Permits and privileges, building

Refrigeration system

Retaining walls

Screens

Sidewalks, pavement and driveways on building grounds

Sprinkling systems

Storage facilities constituting part of building

Storage tanks

Structures, cost of

Subways, area ways, and tunnels directly to and forming part of a structure

Vaults, constructed as part of the building

Water supply system for building

Window shades and ventilators

1221   Revenue Equipment

This includes the cost of all units of revenue passenger equipment and the cost of the first set of accessory equipment necessary to make them ready for service, excluding tires and tubes. If purchased in a condition ready for service, the cost shall include the invoice or contract price (excluding tires and tubes). It may also include the cost of spare engines and other major units carried on hand for maintenance purposes. Items in this account are defined as:

Automobiles

Buses

Combination buses

Horses and mules

Stages

It can be seen that this uniform system of accounts originated in the early 1900s.

1251   Furniture and Office Equipment

This account includes the cost of furniture and appliances used in general offices, garages, stations, terminals, warehouses, and waiting rooms, when equipment is not an integral part of the housing structure. Records of such equipment must be maintained by each location. If a carrier operates or owns auxiliary station facilities, such as restaurants and newsstands, the cost at those locations must be separated under a special subdivision entitled furniture and office equipment—special facilities.

Items included in this account are:

Bookcases

Cash registers

Chairs, stools, and benches

Clocks

Counters

Desks

Equipment in rest, dining, recreation, and medical rooms

Fans, electric

Filing cabinets

Fire extinguisher equipment

Floor coverings

Heaters and lamps (movable)

Kitchen equipment

Lighting fixtures (movable)

Lockers

Loudspeaker systems

Newsstand equipment

Office equipment (mechanical)

Parcel room equipment

Partitions and railings

Restaurant equipment

Safes (movable)

Showcases and shelves

Tables and counters

Teletypewriters

Ticket cases

Ticket machines

Time clocks

Time-table racks

Typewriters

Vacuum cleaners

Water coolers

NOTE: Small articles of slight value or of short life may be charged to the appropriate expense account.

10

GOVERNMENT ACCOUNTING

INTRODUCTION

There are a number of differences in the way businesses and governments use generally accepted accounting practices. The accounting for property, plant, and equipment, and other long-term capital assets is the most diverse between government and business.

The basis for business accounting is the accrual method, and coupled with it, the need to establish the value of assets and liabilities. The current net worth of a business is an important aspect of most business measurement plans. The annual financial reports are the basis for analyzing the impact of each year's activities on that net worth. The accrual accounting system also provides the means to match the revenues generated in the business cycle and the expenses by time period. A typical business must raise capital through either bank borrowings or public offering of stock or bonds. In order to be competitive in those markets, measurements have been developed over the years. Average return on investment and debt to equity ratios are important to business financing activities.

Government, however, rarely finances based on asset values. Typically, the voters are asked to pass a bond issue or capital assets are financed out of one year's operations (tax revenue).

FUND ACCOUNTING

Government accounting has grown around the concept of fund accounts. A fund to a business would be a separate company. A fund in government accounting is a separate set of accounts and records for another entity. The general fund of a government entity is similar to the company's general ledger accounts. However, there are also other funds, such as enterprise funds for businesses governments operate and trust funds, maintained to ensure that dedicated revenues are used for the purpose intended. These make up a unique general fixed assets and liabilities group.

The general fund normally does not contain any property, plant, or equipment, the only assets maintained in the general fund are those related to specific property funds or trust funds. All other assets are accounted for in a general fixed assets group.

The general fixed assets group (GFAG) is not really a fund, but is an off-book ledger of long-term assets. This account group is maintained to keep a record of the original cost of assets purchased and placed in service.

INFRASTRUCTURE ASSETS

Government accounting principles have maintained that long-term fixed assets that cannot be sold and used in current operations, are not appropriate to be maintained in either the general fund or the general fixed assets group. These are roads, sidewalks, rights of way, water systems, sewers, and other assets that are unique to government and could not be used for other purposes or typically converted to cash.

Maintaining a record of infrastructure assets is optional. If any record of these assets is maintained, it would be kept in the general fixed assets group along with the other property, plant, and equipment.

As a result of these government accounting rules, most governments in the United States maintain no physical asset records. The records that do exist are limited to the historical costs maintained in the GFAG. All of the costs for these items were charged in some single year. There is no requirement to measure performance. No depreciation is typically charged and cost accounting systems typically do not include assets, but are only concerned with direct marginal costs.

The government accounting policies are based on the belief that asset costs are only part of profit determinations in business. Because government is not involved in establishing a profit (with the exception of enterprise activities), there is no need for establishing the current year's costs of using assets. Further, the "measurement" focus of government funds precludes including depreciation in current operation costs. The accounting focus is on current expendable resources.

The interest rates of financing government bonds are typically not a function of net assets. Nor are they guaranteed by the mortgage value on those assets. The general credit of government is established based on its ability to collect taxes, not the asset values. The asset value is rarely used as collateral for any debt. As a result of these differences, there has been no historical need to keep government records of property, plant, and equipment.

FUNDING FOR GOVERNMENT ASSETS

Government accounting has been based on the principle of cash accounting. It's a "pay as you go" plan. However, this has raised the question of who pays. Should it be the current taxpayers, future taxpayers, or the users of the service (cost causers)? Also, this type of accounting has produced an even greater attitude than in business of "use it up" when managing property, plant, and equipment. There is no comparison maintained of asset value versus outstanding liabilities. Whereas business may be hard pressed to incur debt greater than its total assets, government is restricted only by its capacity to collect taxes. There is also no record to show whether borrowings are financing current consumption or whether they are used to acquire assets of benefit to the future.

ACCOUNTING STANDARD SETTING

The Government Accounting Standards Board (GASB) was established as an independent standard-setting group in 1984. The Financial Accounting Foundation (FAF) is the financing organization for both the Financial Accounting Standards Board, which establishes GAAP for business, and the Government Accounting Standards Board.

In establishing the GASB, the proposed mission was to establish and improve standards of state and local government accounting and financial reporting for the guidance and education of the public, auditors, and users of financial information.

The establishment of the GASB came about as a result of much dissatisfaction with the manner in which government accounting and financial reporting measured the performance of government entities.

The GASB in its initial statements restated past government accounting practice. This included the concept of restricting property, plant, and equipment to the separate general fixed assets group and allowing government the option of not reporting infrastructure assets which are "immovable and of value only to the government unit."

However, the GASB in its first concept statement pointed out a number of factors that would bring about changes in government accounting. Emphasis was placed on the need for public accountability in government through financial reporting. Control mechanisms were needed to ensure the assets were used as intended and that government had a commitment to maintain capital assets so that they will continue to provide service notwithstanding their lack of revenue generation.

The ability of a government entity to delay maintenance on assets needs to be considered in financial reporting objectives. A comparison was made that in a business entity, failing to maintain assets is likely to reduce the revenue stream. Some means of providing a measurement of government's efficiency in maintenance or deferred maintenance was appropriate.

The GASB emphasized that financial reports must assist in evaluating efficiency and effectiveness. In order to have accountability of a government entity, it is necessary that citizens be able to evaluate their government. The Board also stated its belief that there needed to be some assurances that debt will be repaid before the assets purchased are no longer usable. The GASB also raised the issue of interperiod equity. The Board emphasized that interperiod equity must exist. There should not be a shifting of the current budget to future-year taxpayers. Interperiod equity is described as the significant part of accountability. Nothing material can be omitted from the financial reports. But how can interperiod equity exist without making an assessment of deferred maintenance and the cost of using up assets (depreciation)? The GASB points out that some of these measures of government efficiencies and effectiveness may need some measurement other than dollars, and suggests that a measurement such as miles of road repaired might be such a solution.

MEASURING SERVICE EFFORTS AND ACCOMPLISHMENTS

The GASB has established a service efforts and accomplishments project. The purpose is to establish a measurement of efficiency and productiveness in government. The project proposes to establish measurements of government that have not existed before. These measurements proposed are to be based on measuring inputs, outputs, outcomes, or results. This is in contrast to most current self-measurements by government entities, which measure in terms of activities, not in terms of the number of goals accomplished. The purposes of these new measurements would be to report categories in terms of efficiency. There have been proposals made for service efforts and accomplishment efforts for schools, fire services, and sewer systems. The measurements would be based on units of accomplishments such as miles of road repaired or fires extinguished, as well as ratios of percentage of assets maintained in the current year. The GASB has also concluded that there is no major difference in financial reporting objectives between government and business activities. Financial reports of government entities must allow determination of whether each year's revenues are sufficient to cover that year's services. As a result of these directions and investigations, it is likely that future government accounting practices will require more emphasis on record keeping for property, plant, and equipment.

CURRENT GOVERNMENT GAAP
PROPERTY RECORDS

Property records are required by government entities to establish control and fix responsibility for asset custody. Within a government entity, accountability and stewardship of assets owned is even greater for the government manager than for the business manager. Without control mechanisms and identification of property, that stewardship cannot be efficiently carried out.

The effective use of a property that is currently owed by a government agency must be assured. A property record allows an organized approach and maintains a record of current usage and maintenance and provides for future replacement. The property record can be the basis for a capital budgeting plan to provide for replacement of property, plant, and equipment.

The property record is needed to establish reasonable amounts of insurance coverage and to establish insurance claims subsequent to a loss. The property record also provides that minimal security necessary against pilferage of vulnerable equipment. When equipment is not even missed because there is no record to prove its existence, assets may be lost.

MEASUREMENT OF UTILIZATION

Schools typically are in session 182 days out of the year. If that is the only use of the physical plant, it is less than 50 percent of the days and 33 percent of the hours available. A property record including buildings, rooms, and utilization can provide the basis for comparison of this year versus last year within the school district. Similarly, comparisons can be made to other districts, where the cost of using up that physical plant is spread over a different life.

School managers have begun finding ways to get greater utilization from their assets. A number of schools operate on a year-round basis with either one-third or one-fourth of the students on vacation at any given time. Evening programs of adult education also provide greater utilization of school facilities. Multi-purpose rooms or auditoriums may be provided to community organizations during non-school hours. Another growing service is to provide child care on the school site for before and after school periods.

The state of California has provided an incentive to local districts to adopt some means of year-round use of their school buildings. They did this by giving priority to those districts that have year-round use when considering appliclations for state aid to the construction of new school buildings. The Government Accounting Standards Board (GASB) is currently considering establishing specific measurement ratios that will consider, among other things, utilization of school facilities.

Similarly it has been estimated that courtrooms in the United States are used from 10 percent to 20 percent of the time. A property record of courtrooms with past utilization records and reservations systems could provide the means for more efficient use.

As in business, the government manager needs information to plan, schedule, and monitor performance improvements. Performance improvements includes the reducing of cost to provide service. Indirect costs make up the major portion of government cost. The cost of using up assets is one of those costs. Depreciation is a measure of the consumption of resources purchased with prior period dollars. Other events requiring the use of a property record are the cost systems that provide a recovery system from users. Government is moving more and more to fees for service. These include the cost of arresting drunk drivers, review of developers proposed plans, and inspections of premises by fire, health, and other officials. In order to establish government costs for these services, the asset costs must be included. In addition to justifying fees, management of the facilities require full costing systems. For example, what is the difference in cost for using portable classrooms in schools versus constructing physical plants that will last thirty years or more?

All of this is coming to a head now as areas have rapid growth and no longer can finance based on selling more bonds. When growth occurs in a community, who should pay for the additional infrastructure? Is it enough to replace wornout, undermentioned property, or is it necessary to provide for the new development?

ESTABLISHING PROPERTY RECORD

The chapters in this book that provide guidance for preparing property records for business are equally applicable to government. However, there are some unique requirements of government that

139

are not necessary for many businesses. The record-keeping necessary for buildings, most equipment, and vehicles, are the same.

Where government provides many miles of roads, sidewalks, sewers, and storm drains, different accounting problems exist.

ESTABLISHING PROPERTY RECORD UNITS

Property record units must be established in designing a property record. They are typically a single vehicle, groups of furniture, and individual pieces of machinery. Each property record unit will have a separate record and be individually identified within the property record information database.

INFRASTRUCTURE PROPERTY UNITS

It is necessary to establish some unit for measurement, such as per thousand feet for continuous structures like roads and sidewalks. Although this poses a problem for government not existing in most business, it is identical to the problem of continuous structure such as railroads and public utility wire systems. Public utilities typically use thousands of feet or wire miles as a property record unit. In establishing property records for infrastructures, an entity would do well to use either units of thousands of feet or miles. A number of jurisdictions have established public utility property records for their enterprise ventures. Government entities that operate electric utilities are required to maintain them in accordance with business GAAP.

Because there has not been a requirement to maintain property records in the past, a substantial undertaking will be necessary to obtain all of the information.

PLANNING

The necessity for establishing a careful plan before attempting to carry out a goal cannot be emphasized enough. The plan should contain a list of tasks which must be accomplished, who is going to perform them, and the time required to complete each task. A partial list of activities will include:

Designing or selecting property record information system

Establishing property record units

Locating and inventorying the existing property units

Establishing original cost of units

Assessing cost of deferred maintenance

Establishing accounting policies

Designing coding systems

Establishing reports needed

Designing input forms

ACCOUNTING POLICIES

When establishing property record units, a number of accounting policy issues will be raised, including the minimum capitalization value. Businesses typically establish a rate of either $500, $1,000, or $5,000 as a minimum capitalization rate. Group purchases such as a cafeteria of furniture may use those amounts for the entire group. This decision should not be taken lightly, as it will have a major impact on the ability to establish and maintain the property record. Having too large a unit eliminates control. However, cost benefit should be kept in mind and detailed records are costly. Some jurisdictions have established that unit costs will be more than $15,000. However, certain units are all kept, such as buildings, vehicles, computers. Whereas business GAAP calls for capitalization of items with a life longer than one year, government currently has more latitude. A number of jurisdictions have established two years as the minimum life for capitalization. Items with an estimated life of two years are considered operating expenses. The federal government and the military typically classify items used by only one person as expendable and property records are not maintained.

SOFTWARE SELECTION

Requirements to obtain approval from a governing body through a bid process will increase the complexities for most governments. After the system has been designed and these characteristics documented, the process of identifying vendors can begin. Small entities with only a few thousand property record units may be able to use existing off-the-shelf software. If so, an analysis similar to that outlined for business is appropriate. Many government agencies, however, will find it necessary to identify a list of vendors whose existing software or experience at producing packages is a probable match with the agency's needs. A request for information should be sent to those vendors outlining the design and services required. The vendor's proposal for service should include a plan that shows how they will meet the definition requirements, including maintenance of the record and provision for infrastructure assets. Where an existing computer system is intended for use, the vendor should be notified. Analysis of the response should be made, narrowing the list to a few vendors before detailed analysis is done.

In selecting a vendor, emphasis should be on their willingness to meet the agency's requirements, as well as on establishing their competence. Visiting past satisfied customers and reviewing their systems may be time well spent.

From the information gained, a specific bid proposal can be established if necessary.

The government accountant would do well to follow procedure outlined for business except where specific unique circumstances require otherwise.

11

NOT-FOR-PROFIT ACCOUNTING

INTRODUCTION

Few areas of accounting have less documentation and more confusing accounting requirements than not-for-profit organizations. The first problem is agreeing to a definition of not-for-profit and sorting out the many different terms applied.

Not-for-profit, nonprofit, tax-exempt, and charitable are terms sometimes used to describe an organization. The first problem is to clearly distinguish between these terms which come from accounting, tax, and popular use. In defining not-for-profit, the intent, not necessarily the results, must be considered. Many businesses that are organized for the purpose of providing goods or services with a return or profit to their owners do not accomplish that goal. They may even be able to maintain themselves in business over an extended period of time without generating a profit. Generally, this is accomplished by using up the assets that were initially dedicated to the business.

Similarly, organizations that are created to provide services and have no intent to make a profit do so on some of their activities.

The Internal Revenue Service (IRS) regulations pertain to tax-exempt organizations. An organization may qualify for exemption from Federal Income Tax if it is organized and operated exclusively for charitable, religious, educational, scientific, or literary purposes or for testing for public safety or the fostering of international amateur sports competition. In order to qualify for tax exemption, the organization must be a corporation or a community chest, fund, or foundation. A trust is a fund or foundation and may qualify. However, an individual or partnership will never qualify for tax exemption purposes. One of the not-for-profit organization treasurer's responsibilities is to ensure that the organization's responsibilities as to tax-exempt status are maintained. Numerous IRS publications exist to describe the process for obtaining and maintaining tax-exempt status. Because of their volatility, the reader should obtain the current appropriate IRS publications to determine current requirements.

ACCOUNTING DEFINITION OF NOT-FOR-PROFIT ORGANIZATIONS

The Financial Accounting Standards Board in issuing Concept Statement IV addressed a definition for nonbusiness organizations. It defines such an organization as:

a. Receipts of significant amounts of resources from resource providers who do not expect to receive either repayment or economic benefits proportionate to resources provided

b. Operating purposes that are primarily other than to provide goods or services at a profit or profit equivalent

c. Absence of defined ownership interests that can be sold, transferred, or redeemed, or that convey entitlement to a share of a residual distribution of resources in the event of liquidation of the organization

There are a great many not-for-profit organizations. Most are small, however many are among the world's largest organizations. Universities, health care organizations, and churches are among some of the largest organizations in existence. Similarly, associations and professional societies, particularly membership organizations, range from a few members to tens of thousands. These organizations provide all types of services. Examples are:

Associations and professional societies

Colleges and universities

Health care providers

Libraries

Museums

Schools

Social services providers

Typically, these organizations are managed by a volunteer board of directors. The directors are elected if a membership organization or replacements are appointed by the board in total as vacancies occur. One of these directors is appointed as the treasurer and accepts fiduciary responsibility for the organization. The fact that this treasurer is a part-time volunteer does not in any way diminish the total responsibility for the stewardship of the organization's assets. In larger organizations, executive directors, bookkeepers, and public accounting firms may be employed to assist in accomplishing the tasks.

To review the entire responsibilities of accounting for not-for-profit organizations, the reader is referred to another John Wiley publication, *Financial and Accounting Guide for Not-for-Profit Organizations* by Malvern J. Gross, Jr. The authors of that book explain:

The treasurer has significant responsibilities, including the following:
1. Keeping financial records.
2. Preparing accurate and meaningful financial statements.
3. Budgeting and anticipating financial problems.
4. Safeguarding and managing the organization's financial assets.
5. Complying with Federal and State reporting requirements.

While this list certainly is not all-inclusive, most of the financial problems the treasurer will face are associated with these five major areas.

Three of these areas pertain to the accounting and safeguarding of property, plant, and equipment. This discussion will be limited to the area of property, plant, and equipment as it applies to keeping financial records, safeguarding and maintaining those assets, and providing accurate and meaningful financial statements allowing the board to exercise its stewardship responsibilities of these physical assets.

145

ACCOUNTING PROBLEMS OF
NOT-FOR-PROFIT ORGANIZATIONS

Donations are the major source of capital for asset purchases. Grants and donations are often designated for the specific purpose of accomplishing capital projects. Indeed, specific land or building construction projects may be defined before the grant or donation is solicited. A number of major donors may provide "donor-restricted" funds for such things as church or school building improvements or a fund for the maintenance of those buildings.

Typically, not-for-profit organizations use cash accounting. Their assets are purchased with grants or donations for special fund drives. There is no impact on current operating statements as a result of receipt of these donations and their use in purchasing or constructing property, plant, or equipment. Only when one of these assets is destroyed or lost may it affect current operations. Another problem is the difficulty of most board members in understanding depreciation.

During the formative years and until very recently, no real accounting rules existed for nonprofit organizations. Only public accountants involved in a very specialized accounting practice dealt with not-for-profit organizations. Indeed, much of the accounting services were provided pro bono by individual certified public accountants as a public service. In reviewing the accounting literature, one will find that most GAAP guides do not even have not-for-profit or nonprofit in their indexes. Those that do limit most of their discussion to the relatively recent FASB releases.

The management of not-for-profit organizations is similar to management of government. Therefore fund accounting as defined in government publications has extensive use within these organizations. That is, a general fund is used for current operating revenues and expenses. A separate capital asset fund may be maintained. However, many organizations only maintain the capital asset fund to substantiate a fund drive and identify how those funds have been converted to physical assets. No attempt is made to maintain the capital asset fund.

The prevailing theory is that assets are purchased by special fund drives, they are put in place and will be used. At the end of their useful life or when major renovations are required another fund drive will be undertaken. That makes it a future problem and not one of consequence to the current board of directors or treasurer. When needed, it will be a current year short-term drive when the major resources of the organization will be turned to raising the funds to construct new facilities.

FORMAL ACCOUNTING STANDARDS

A number of formal documents have been issued by the FASB regarding not-for-profit organizations in recent years. Concept Statement VI was issued in 1985 and began defining what constitutes a not-for-profit or nonprofit business organization. A great deal of controversy has surrounded the FASB Statement on Depreciation, SFAS 93 issued in August 1987. This Statement requires that physical assets be capitalized and depreciated over their lives and reported on external financial statements of not-for-profit organizations.

Further, a proposal on financial statement presentations was issued in May of 1991 requiring the reporting of net property, plant, and equipment as an asset on external financial statements. There is a requirement for the capitalization of art and historical treasures also.

A proposal has been recently issued regarding the accounting for contributions and was in the review stages in early 1993.

In spite of these official pronouncements requiring capitalization and depreciation by not-for-profit organizations, it has not had a major impact on the accounting, nor on the financial reports of most organizations. Many not-for-profit institutions, even large ones, just live with the qualified statement by the auditor that the statements do not meet generally accepted accounting practices as pertain to the accounting for physical assets and depreciation. A large number of smaller not-for-profits do not subject their financial statements to an external audit and attestation.

NEED FOR CHANGE IN NOT-FOR-PROFIT ACCOUNTING

There are a number of changes occurring that increase the need for audited financial statements of not-for-profit organizations and an attestation that the organization is following generally accepted accounting principles.

Not-for-profit organizations are getting larger and have more paid staff. These include many career not-for-profit managers who bring more expertise and training to their jobs. These organizations are also providing greater numbers of services than ever before.

Provision of many of the services by not-for-profit organizations are financed either by government, tax grants, or cost reimbursement contracts. There is also more competition for the fewer donations available. Large donors are demanding more accountability for the funds provided and demand both letters of determination from the IRS as to tax-exempt status and audited financial statements that attest the organization's use of generally accepted accounting principles in reporting their financial activities. Thus, as the formal accounting rules are being promulgated requiring recognition of physical assets, the sources of funding for these organizations are demanding that they follow the accounting principles and practices as promulgated by the standard setting bodies.

Additionally, there is a requirement for improved management controls. As the organizations grow in both size and complexity, all of the pressures existing on business and government entities come to play in the not-for-profit organization. Now, many have part-time managers; the volunteer treasurer from the board of directors is no longer able to oversee the accounting process without professional assistance. In addition, the cost of many items is getting much greater. The organization is dependent upon expensive, small, and portable items that require control. Examples of these items are:

Copiers

Computers

Cellular telephones

Facsimile machines

Motor vehicles

Office equipment

Televisions and video players

Also, cost accounting systems must provide information allowing the collection of fees for the reimbursement of services provided. Typically, the person obtaining the services does not pay for them. But increasingly, social and health services are being provided by not-for-profit organizations and they are reimbursed for the cost of these services by government organizations. Thus the cost accounting systems need to include the cost of using up assets (depreciation). Cost accounting reports must allow the board of directors and treasurer to ensure that reimbursement for services covers all of the cost. In addition, the pricing of cooperative ventures by not-for-profit organizations requires review of total cost. The justification of non-profit status to the IRS requires inclusion of all costs in financial reports. All organizations have invested in some amounts of property, plant, and equipment. To not maintain records of that cost and acknowledge the using up of assets during subsequent accounting periods will result in insufficient revenues to cover costs. Although the intent of a not-for-profit organization is not to make a profit, it must, over a period of time, recover all of its costs in some fashion or face the deterioration of its ability to provide services as it uses up its assets. Because of the increasing cost of replacements of such assets, it will be more and more difficult to conduct special fund drives to obtain sufficient donations for large-scale projects.

ACCOUNTING FOR PROPERTY, PLANT, AND EQUIPMENT

Accounting for assets by not-for-profit organizations is changing. The trend is moving toward the same accounting principles as are used by business organizations. Establishing physical property records using the principles outlined in the other chapters of this text will meet generally accepted accounting principles as outlined for not-for-profit organizations. However, it is appropriate now to review the specific accounting pronouncements issued by the FASB outlining some differences.

Concept Statement 6 outlines a definition of net assets of not-for-profit organizations:

90. In a not-for-profit organization, as in a business enterprise, net assets (equity) is a residual, the difference between the entity's assets and

its liabilities but, in contrast to equity of a business enterprise, it is not an ownership.

91. Net assets of NFP organizations is divided into three mutually exclusive classes, permanently restricted net assets, temporarily restricted net assets, and restricted net assets.

As in business, assets are purchased, the using up over several periods is recognized in depreciation expense. This provides the basis for consideration of the specialized accounting principles of not-for-profit (NFP) organizations.

Unless a not-for-profit organization maintains its net assets, its ability to continue to provide services dwindles; either future providers must make up the deficiency or services to future beneficiaries will decline. Deferred maintenance is a real cost.

In order to produce financial statements including assets and the residual difference between assets and liabilities (net worth) records must be established of the current value of all assets. The correct way to accomplish this is by establishing a property record.

Another FASB Statement, SFAS 32, outlines appropriate industry accounting practices for not-for-profit organizations providing those services. A partial list includes:

AICPA audit guides

Audits of certain nonprofit organizations

Audits of voluntary health and welfare organizations

Audits of providers of health care services

These audit guides all outline the requirement to maintain records of physical assets and depreciate them.

The FASB, in issuing Statement 93, Recognition of Depreciation by Not-for-Profits, intended to settle an ongoing argument as to whether or not depreciation was a valid expense for notprofit organizations. This statement formalizes the requirement that depreciation expense must be recognized in order for the financial statements issued by a not-for-profit organization to meet GAAP.

There is a requirement to capitalize and depreciate on some equitable basis (similar to business depreciation in Chapter 8). The reasons given in this statement are a need by the beneficiaries, board, management, and others to be able to obtain information on inflows and outflows of resources and the relations between those flows. Further, there is a need for information about service efforts and accomplishments. How can the accomplishments of a not-for-profit organization be measured without consideration of all costs? The use of physical assets decreases their future usefulness. This decline in usefulness must be recognized in measuring the accomplishments and services provided by an organization.

To make an assessment of how well managers discharge their stewardship responsibilities, an accounting for physical assets is necessary. Just as cash on hand or in the bank needs to be safeguarded, so do the buildings, furniture, and other property, plant, and equipment assets.

Donated assets are required to be recognized at fair market value on the date of receipt. Depreciation of donated assets is as valid a cost over their life as assets purchased with donated money. These long-lived assets provide benefit to a not-for-profit organization as well as they would to a business over several periods. This results in cost for the services provided during those future periods.

Although some not-for-profit organizations are ignoring either the requirement for a formal audit or obtaining qualified statements because of their not maintaining asset records, that should not be the practice.

CREATING PROPERTY RECORDS

When the decision has been made to maintain property records for physical assets, the principles are the same as outlined in this book for a business entity. However, there are a few differences that will be discussed here.

In a business organization, the accounting classification is normally accomplished by nonaccountants. The same is true of not-for-profit organizations. In addition, it should be emphasized that greater simplicity may be needed in the nonprofit organization because the asset control may be done using part-time volunteers. A complex process is not likely to be understood or followed. Also, the treasurer and board of directors may have greater direct involvement with this process than is true in business organizations. Therefore, in making every decision, simplicity and straightforward procedures should be emphasized.

The first step in the establishment is to set an expense limit, because there is a cost benefit relationship that needs to be considered. The smaller the expense limit, the greater the record keeping and the less return on the cost and effort. Most organizations establish expense limits of either $1,000 or $500. For a small not-for-profit organization with few physical assets, a $100 expense limit may be appropriate. Organizations using mostly volunteers have an even greater problem in keeping track of where their assets are. Some not-for-profit organizations do not have offices or specific places of business. They conduct their organization's activities in borrowed quarters and store physical assets in between use at members' homes or businesses. When this is the case, a lowered expense limit or a property record that contains expense items may be appropriate to provide adequate control of equipment.

An expense limit of $1,000, for example, would be greater than the cost of video cameras, typewriters, and perhaps portable computers. It is highly encouraged that either a lower expense limit be set or the property record be established to capture the existence and status of expensed items between $100 and $1,000.

In establishing the property record when one has not existed in the past, historical cost may not be available. If that is the case, there are simple ways to estimate the costs that are appropriate. A cost-based appraisal could be made using either professional appraisers or a sampling of the current market. With automobiles, the "blue book" values can be considered. For equipment where there is a readily available used market, those provide means to establish a current appraisal.

Replacement cost could be established by pricing new items. If the cost of the item is established by reviewing replacement cost, it would then be appropriate to reduce that cost by the estimated depreciation appropriate from the approximate date of acquisition. Again, acquisition date may be estimated.

Property tax assessments are available. Some states also levy personal property taxes on business property (as opposed to real property taxes). The tax assessor's records, where they are itemized in detail, may be used to estimate the original cost for the items. Care should be taken in using these tax records for that purpose, however, because of the difference of opinion of tax assessors and other appraisers. Assessments for tax purposes may be on a percentage relationship on actual value and is a means for generating revenue on some reasonable basis across business entities.

The other caution to raise here for treasurers of not-for-profit organizations is the fulfilling of the responsibility to pay taxes. There is much confusion as to when an organization is exempt from federal income tax. An exempt organization is just that, exempt from federal income taxes. The same organization may or may not be exempt from state income taxes, real property taxes, and personal property taxes. In fact, some organizations will be subjected to the normal business taxes for any asset that is not used for the charitable or exempt purpose of the organization. For example, in the state of California religious organizations are exempt from real estate taxes, as are schools. However, buildings and real property used for housing of clergy are not exempt and property tax is assessed on those areas. Similarly, counties may assess a tax on plant and equipment as well. In fulfilling their stewardship responsibilities, the board of directors and specifically the treasurer of a not-for-profit organization must understand and comply with various local tax laws.

PROPERTY RECORD

The property record needs to be maintained in a flexible manner. A large organization will put the property record on a computer. A small organization may find that an index card file for their few assets is appropriate. In creating the record, it is important to be able to modify the changeable information simply. In an index card system, a pencil and eraser at the location of the file and a custodian may suffice. A new card should be created when the old one is worn out. Following are examples of the information that should be contained in the property record. In addition, review Chapter 12, "Creation and Verification of Property Records," to see whether the elements needed by business organizations are also appropriate.

Description

Include in the description information adequate to identify the item.

Inventory terminology like "one each typewriter, electric, blue, IBM" is not always the best description.

Cost

Historical cost either based on purchase documents or estimated is needed.

Means of Establishing Cost

Enter into the record whether the cost was established from purchase documents appraisals or replacement costs. This will be important in establishing a record for the organization, as well as for entering items that are donated.

Date of Acquisition

This is the date that the organization puts the asset into service, either after purchase or after receiving it as a donation.

Location

If the item is kept in a building or location under the control of the organization, a simple address or code will suffice. However, where the not-for-profit organization maintains its physical assets on the premises of others, a more precise location description may be required, for example, "in member Smith's barn loft," with address.

Custodian

The person who has actually assumed responsibility for the custody and care of the item should be identified. This may be the member who is storing it between activities or the person using it on a daily basis.

Property Tax Information (Real or Personal)

Establish with local tax assessor the appropriate tax status of each item. Generally, groups of items like office equipment either will be subject or will not be subject to tax. Referring to lists may eliminate the requirement for review of each item by the tax assessor.

Vendor

If the item was purchased, the vendor it was purchased from as opposed to the manufacturer (which is included in the description) should be identified here.

Donor

Donated items should include identification of the person or organization that donated the item.

Restrictions on Use of the Property, If Any

Property that is donated for a particular service or use should be identified here. Real estate or buildings may actually revert to the donor if they are not continued in their intended use. Many cities and not-for-profit organizations have discovered that the Carnegie Library buildings built sixty or seventy years ago must continue to be used for library purposes; they cannot be sold and the proceeds used for some other purpose.

Depreciation Method

Identify the depreciation method.

Expected Remaining Life

Each year, or at least periodically, an inventory should be taken to establish the item's continued existence and an assessment made as to how long it can continue to provide its intended service. Reviewing the status of physical assets on a regular basis is important in establishing future capital budgets and planning for replacements.

Future Usefulness

Equipment used by not-for-profit organizations may have use only while the specific service or activity is continued. Similarly, items that have long since been discontinued in business organizations because of their obsolescence may continue to be used in not-for-profit organizations. Examples of these are adding machines and typewriters, as opposed to computers and word processors. An assessment and record of how the item may be useful to the organization would be appropriate during the physical inventory.

SYSTEM DOCUMENTATION

Accountants establishing property records for not-for-profit organizations need to be particularly concerned with the documentation of the system.

The nature of not-for-profit organizations causes more volatility in employees and workers than with comparably sized business organizations. Elected treasurers may turn over each year. Members of the board of directors typically serve from one to four years. They may or may not have a formal training process to pick up information from their predecessors. All of these items make it even more important that the property record system be appropriately documented in an asset or accounting manual. Simple checklists that provide direction for the person acquiring a new asset are appropriate.

12

CREATION AND VERIFICATION OF PROPERTY RECORDS

INTRODUCTION

The most important element in successful asset management is a comprehensive single record of all the information necessary about each individual physical asset. This single record becomes a part of the general accounting system. It must be simple to maintain and update in the normal transaction process.

The concept of a single record is important. If more than one record exists, they must constantly be reconciled with each other. However, if by its construction, the subsidiary property record is kept in balance with the general ledger system, this reconciliation step is eliminated. This can be accomplished by using the transaction for general ledger to create a new property record. Perhaps the best way to understand is to look at a specific example. If a new light truck is purchased to be used for transporting products, there will be an invoice created in order to pay for that purchase. The document that creates the requirement for payment should also include the accounting information necessary for property record update. The motor vehicle provides us with the best example because there are many different facets that must be provided for.

Information necessary to the general ledger system and accounts payable include payment, total amount owed, motor vehicle license fees included, and terms of payment (immediate, ten days, net thirty days, etc.). If the property record number, description, date of purchase, and intended use are included on the document, this will allow the creation of a property record also.

The creation of the initial property record with the amount paid for the vehicle, its I.D. number, and a description keeps the ledger record and the property record in balance. Edits in the general ledger system should not allow entry without property record and accounts payable information.

It is not necessary at this time to enter all information about the motor vehicle in the property record, however. For example, the motor vehicle license number is not likely to be known at the time of purchase. This will come at a later date. Having established the initial record of existence of this motor vehicle in the property record provides the means to notify the asset manager that additional information is necessary. The notification should result from the property record update from the general ledger interface.

If the motor vehicle is then taken to a local shop for modification, additional information is necessary. In this example, lets say a hydraulic lift gate is to be added to the back of the pickup. Again, an invoice from the auto shop will be received and must be paid. The payment for the lift gate and its installation should include identification of the motor vehicle it was installed on and the appropriate asset account, if the cost is greater than $1,000. It will cause both the accounts payable system to generate payment and an updated dollar amount to the original cost of the motor vehicle. The lift gate may be an increase to the motor vehicle historical cost or a new property unit may be created. (See Chapter 4, "Determining Base Unit.")

PURPOSE OF PROPERTY RECORD

This property record file will be used to provide information needed to manage the asset. This information will be the basis for knowing about past investments in assets and planning for future ones. By having the date of placement of all the assets, it is possible to establish the average age and make plans for future required purchases. Control of assets includes knowing the location and current-year maintenance expense of each. Appropriate amounts of insurance can be determined from information in the file. It also will provide substantiation for insurance claims. In case of fire, flood, earthquake, or other catastrophe to a building, having a detailed list of physical assets included in the building will provide the means for making an insurance claim.

Where a number of motor vehicles are owned, their annual registration with the state comes due on many different dates. Although some states provide a billing service as a reminder, many do not. Failure to pay registration fees on time can result in significant penalties. Including in the property record the vehicle registration or license number, amount of the prior year's registration fee, and the expiration date, provides the means to produce a report forecasting the subsequent years' required registration payments.

Management needs to know the physical condition and capacity of these physical assets on a periodic basis. When including records of maintenance, it is possible to identify weak assets that should be replaced earlier than would be normal. Other information unique to the particular asset may be appropriate. For example, aircraft are required to have inspections on a regular basis. After each 100 hours of operation and annually, the aircraft must be inspected and maintenance performed on any item found outside acceptable tolerances. Maintaining the date and cost of the previous inspections provides information for forecasting the next one. The cost accounting for aircraft operations should include hours of usage and appropriate costs each month. By maintaining that record of hours of use, it is possible to ensure that the next 100-hour inspection is accomplished on time. Also, it is appropriate to forecast the inspection to avoid times when the aircraft will be needed. The aircraft may be out of service for a week or more for the inspection and maintenance.

Similarly, although not required by law, it is possible to maintain a schedule for maintenance of production facilities in a manufacturing plant. The pieces of machinery in a production line can have future maintenance requirements identified based on past records. By including within the property record a forecast of future maintenance, this work can be scheduled during a time when the production facility is not needed.

NEW CONCEPT

Managing assets through the use of a database has not been done by most companies in the past. The need for better product quality and the greater cost of physical assets has caused a reexamination of these factors. There is now an even higher demand that a production line's regular maintenance is within tolerance and that the line is capable of producing quality products. High cost of many assets, as well as the cost of financing them, requires that each business get the best use out of its physical assets in order to be competitive.

Also, the advent of inexpensive but powerful computers has provided the means to store the great amounts of information that are necessary to manage physical assets.

Although these records, theoretically, could be kept manually in a small business, computer records will be necessary for most. Pre-programmed "off-the-shelf" packages for maintaining computer asset records within a general ledger system are available. These range from very expensive systems that can be tailored for the individual company to packages available for less than $1,000, which are adequate for most small firms. Complete systems are discussed in Chapter 13, "Computer Programs."

The remainder of this chapter will discuss the details of establishing an asset database. The assumption is that it will be accomplished on a computer, however, records can just as easily be maintained manually if there are only a few assets. The principles that will be discussed are the same, whether the information is stored in a manual file folder for each individual asset or is stored on a computer, which can handle the information more efficiently for large numbers of records. In fact, even the largest business must still have a manual file folder of some sort for each asset that has paper that must be preserved. For example, deeds and easement documents for property and buildings must be maintained in a file, as well as certificates of ownership of motor vehicles and similar assets.

REQUIREMENTS FOR A PHYSICAL ASSET DATABASE

The information that is needed within the asset database includes:

1. Property record identification number
2. Account code
3. Subaccount code
4. Location code
5. Property record category number
   Land
   Land improvement
   Buildings
   Motor vehicles
      State vehicle license number
      Manufacturer vehicle identification number
      Registration fee
   Furniture
   Production equipment
   Computers
6. Description of property record item
   Passenger automobile
7. Dollar amounts
   Original cost
   Cost of additions
   Current market value/date value established
   Insurance value/date value established
   Maintenance by year
   Accumulated depreciation
8. Usage
   Mileage, date (tachometer)
   Hours of use (hour meter)

By having an integrated general ledger and asset management systems, there is a positive control when an invoice is paid with a

	Item 1	Item 2	Item 3
Property Record ID	PCoo15		
General Ledger Account	13301		
Sub Account	112		
Location Code	421 East Lansing		
Category	PC		
License #			
Description	PC CPU		
Original Cost	$2,584		
Additions	$831		
Current Value	$3,415		
Insurance Value	$3,000		
Mileage			
Hours (Hobbs meter)			

FIGURE 12.1   Property record information—input document.

capital account involved. It is not necessary to code the original invoice with all of the above information, however; it is possible to include only the property record identification number and the dollar amount at point of payment. This allows the property record management system to create a new record for the item and the dollar amounts so it will balance in the ledger. It is desirable, though, to capture as much information as possible initially. In many cases, all of the information on the document can be coded before the invoices are paid. This coding on the original document should be the responsibility of the purchasing department and they should have detailed instructions in the asset accounting manual telling them how to code a document. Someone should be assigned as a physical asset manager. He or she will manage the system and answer questions as they arise. This responsibility is best placed in the accounting department and a telephone number should be listed, making that person available to answer questions on purchasing. Unique property may require discussions between the accountant, the purchasing agent, and someone in engineering or production with technical knowledge of what the piece of equipment in question does.

Purchase of an integrated production facility including conveyors and computer-operated milling machines will require many decisions. Which pieces of equipment will require an individual record item and which are included all as one? This is discussed in detail in Chapter 4, "Determining Base Units."

PROPERTY RECORD UNITS

Property record units are the basic items controlled in the asset database. They normally correspond to a base unit, and will be the smallest item individually controlled. It is necessary to code these items with unique serial numbers. Also, it is appropriate to define by categories and location *and other details* so that they may easily be summarized by the computer for reporting purposes. Refer to the chapter on establishing base units in order to review the concept of coding and identifying these individual items.

CODING SYSTEMS

Coding systems should be created in accordance with the parameters given in the computer asset management package. Many industries have recommended coding systems for their members. Real estate, utilities, and government organizations are typical examples of industries where established industry coding systems exist.

A good property record coding system will have sufficient fields and digits to encode all of the information necessary in numeric format. In the selection of an asset management property record system ensure that it has sufficient field length to allow for all coding required in your company. A good length would be fifteen digits total that can be identified as separate fields by the user. By identifying separate fields within this property record number, report making is facilitated.

The concepts outlined above are best understood through reviewing an example; see the following property record-coding system used for motor vehicles.

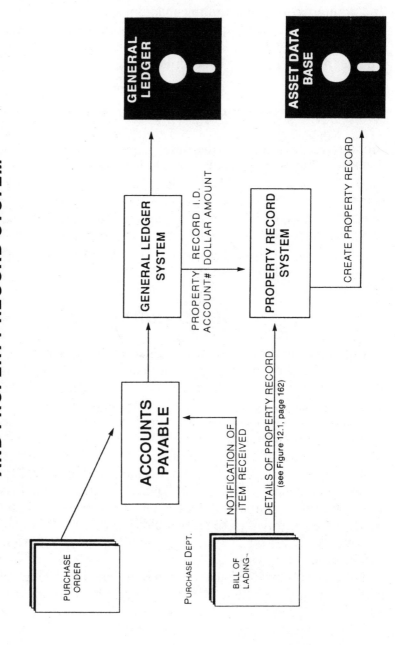

DATA FLOW FOR INTEGRATED LEDGER AND PROPERTY RECORD SYSTEM

PURCHASE ORDER

PURCHASE DEPT.

BILL OF LADING-

ACCOUNTS PAYABLE

NOTIFICATION OF ITEM RECEIVED

DETAILS OF PROPERTY RECORD
(see Figure 12.1, page 162)

GENERAL LEDGER SYSTEM

GENERAL LEDGER

PROPERTY RECORD I.D.
ACCOUNT# DOLLAR AMOUNT

PROPERTY RECORD SYSTEM

CREATE PROPERTY RECORD

ASSET DATA BASE

PROPERTY RECORD CODES FOR MOTOR VEHICLES

Property Record Code	Property Record Item
MV	Motor vehicles
MV1	Automobiles
MV11	Motor pool vehicles—sedans
MV12	Motor pool vehicles—station wagons
MV13	Individually assigned automobile
MV20	Light trucks
MV22	Pickups
MV23	Panels
MV24	Pickups with utility beds
MV30	Large trucks
MV31	Tractors
MV32	Refrigerated trailers
MV34	Nonrefrigerated trailers
MV35	Flat bed trailers

By making the code hierarchical in nature, it is possible to select reports using this coding system. For example, looking at the two digits "MV" provides the user with a selection criteria for all motor vehicles. By taking MV1, a selection of small vehicles is called up.

OTHER CODES REQUIRED

A building number code is necessary, along with the floor and a specific location code. This code is probably best assigned including something to identify type of building. For example:

Building Codes

Building Code	Building Type
100	Office buildings
101	14 South Ninth
101201	Rm 201
102	649 Broadway
103	45 Mission

200	Manufacturing plants
210	Sonoma Valley location
211	Plant administration building
212	Firehouse
213	Electronic manufacturing
214	Finished goods warehouse

Organization Code

Organization	Organization Code
A000	Administration
A100	Headquarters, executive level
C000	Controller
C100	Internal auditing
C200	Data processing
C300	Accounts payable
C400	Accounts receivable
C500	General ledger

Location Code

It may be necessary to identify location more precisely than merely a building number or plant address. Examples of this are tax jurisdictions. The individual address may or may not identify specifically the taxing authorities. County or township codes may be required.

PROPERTY RECORD ID NUMBER

This number should be assigned sequentially beginning with one and going through the largest number of items likely to be owned. At least a five-digit number is appropriate. By assigning these numbers sequentially, it is possible to purchase pre-numbered tags that can be permanently affixed to each item. These tags may also be bar coded. Each number would be assigned by the property record manager and included on all documents entered into the accounting system pertaining to that property record unit. This number will be the primary key to the data record database and the complete record can be individually accessed using that number. It facilitates making physical inventories and reporting maintenance on the asset. The tagging of individual items is extremely important in terms of management of the asset. Items that have high value, are relatively small, and can be used for many different purposes need to be tagged for control and security purposes. Office equipment such as personal computers, televisions, VCRs, and sound and projection equipment are particularly vulnerable to loss. These items may be moved from one location to another without notification of the asset manager. When that occurs, they are subject to being "lost" when the next inventory is accomplished.

By attaching an individually assigned number to the item, it is identifiable when found. It is especially important in large companies that have multiple copies of similar items. Without a unique identification number, it would be quite laborious to establish, based on manufacturer's serial number, the actual property record item when a VCR or television was found in a plant other than the one identified in the asset record.

MAINTENANCE OF THE PROPERTY RECORD DATABASE

It is necessary to enter and periodically update information within the property record database. A good technique is to require the reporting documents for the payroll and cost accounting systems to include the ID number of the equipment worked on. When outside agencies perform maintenance on equipment, this should be included on the invoice paying them for their work. That means that the asset database system must be part of not only the general ledger, but also the cost accounting system. If it is not, a second record-keeping system must be established.

The rule in designing systems should be "ONE-WRITE." Whatever document is used to record the time spent for employee payroll should include as much information as possible. Requiring employees to report information on different forms that have nothing to do with the activity being reported will create a massive control problem.

RESPONSIBILITIES OF ASSET MANAGER

It is necessary to have a property record manager who is responsible for ensuring that the property record is maintained. This responsibility in a large organization could be a full-time assignment. In smaller organizations, it is likely to be a collateral duty for one of the staff accountants.

Responsibilities of the property record manager include:

Maintenance of the asset accounting manual

Assignment of property record identification numbers

Maintaining the property record or asset accounting manual

Assisting others in coding asset documents

Being knowledgeable of the asset record-keeping system

Coding unique assets

Assisting with the defining of periodic reports on assets to the data processing organization

Ensuring that periodic sample inventories are conducted by either internal audit or an inventory team

Reviewing periodic reports for missing information in the database and obtaining same

Annual review of insured values of assets

Initiating reports to management identifying cost

Making recommendations for replacement of assets with excessive maintenance requirements

Helping the financial accountant establish new property record classification rules

The property record manager will have more knowledge of this system than anyone else in the company. It is necessary, however, for him or her to work closely with other accounting managers and with upper management to maintain the system.

UPDATING RECORDS

Information placed in the record as a result of normal events in the course of business is the best way to enter information. A major problem exists in the maintenance of location and custodian identification of items that are highly mobile. Video cameras, small computers, and other furniture items are the best examples. Similar problems occur with expensive tools and other portable equipment. There really is no incentive in most businesses to report to the accounting department when a piece of equipment has been moved from one room to another or is being used by a different person. Therefore, some simple scheme of reporting these changes is necessary.

For items that normally move quite a bit, a simple technique to use is similar to that used in a library. Attach to each item a pre-printed card with its I.D. number and a place to write the new location code and custodian identification. This can be sent to the asset manager for entry into the property record system. A new, updated card is then generated and sent to the new custodian for placement on the item. This does not guarantee that every movement or change will be reported, but it makes the process much simpler and therefore increases the likelihood.

Things that move about or are used on a temporary basis, like audiovisual aids used for presentations, can also have special problems. Since it is only for temporary use, the person taking the item intends its return. If the return occurs within a few days there is really no need to update the property records. However, a problem occurs when the intention is not carried out and the item is left in another location.

Each "loan" item should have a standard storage place, so that when it is removed from that location, it is obvious the item is gone. Establishing a central location for storage, instead of each department or manager having a separate space, will make this simpler.

The tool crib approach used in most high school shop classes to ensure that all tools have been replaced at the end of a class period is a good example. It needn't be so elaborate as a hook on the wall with the shape of every tool, but a closet with an empty hole on the shelf will provide the opportunity for a quick review to see whether anything is missing. If a check-out sheet is posted, showing each user, the search for a missing item can be reduced.

RECORDING MAINTENANCE COSTS

Recording physical maintenance of assets on the property record must be automatic. The payment report from the payroll or accounts payable system should generate an interface to the property record system for recording that cost. An example might be the corporate aircraft where, when maintenance is done on an engine, the current-hour reading on that engine and the type of maintenance and cost would be noted in the property record.

Where it is discernable, it is also appropriate to record deferred maintenance. This can be done by an annual assessment of the current state of the equipment. It is not unusual for a maintenance department to create a budget for the coming year. This budget may be prepared by reviewing the kinds of maintenance necessary on a building, for example. Just examining the paint on the exterior of the building may identify that it is beginning to deteriorate and that it would be appropriate to repaint. Also, small areas of fungus or dry rot may be appearing. The total maintenance budget as approved is probably going to be less than the cost of items identified by the maintenance department initially. A typical approach would be to add to the property record a notation under deferred maintenance of those areas recommended for maintenance that are deferred to a later period. This deferred maintenance assessment placed in the property record can give the manager an estimate of future maintenance requirements.

Deferred maintenance can be especially important in assessing why quality has deteriorated or downtime has increased.

VERIFICATION OF PHYSICAL EXISTENCE

In the past it has been typical for an inventory team to be assembled once a year. Armed with a printout from the property record, the team would attempt to locate and verify the physical existence of all items on it. The problem with this approach is that it attempts to pack into a short period of time a task that should be done continuously throughout the year.

Techniques used to determine the physical quantity of units held for sale have been used to establish that property, plant, and equipment still exist. With product inventories, it is a simple matter of identifying and counting everything that exists in a given room and recording it. Inventories of department stores and manufacturing warehouses are examples. The problem with reconciliation of the property, plant, and equipment record with the physical inventory is that a unique item must be found and identified.

The first necessity for identifying items is an easily applied, difficult-to-remove individual serial number affixed to each property record item. Bar coding as well as visual numbers can reduce the effort in verification. Bar coding readers and recorders are now no larger than a small dictation recorder. The inventory can be accomplished by going from room to room reading the bar coded items within each room. It is desirable to have a more sophisticated reader that allows the entry of location code, room number, and custodian I.D. for each location.

MILITARY COMMANDER APPROACH

Where the inventory team is selected for a short task-force type of effort, there is little incentive to be creative and find all of the equipment. A different approach has been adopted by the military. Typically referred to as the "military commander approach," the commander of each military unit is responsible for the physical assets that are shown on the unit's property record. Annually and whenever a change in command occurs, it is necessary to verify the existence of the assets assigned. This is accomplished by trained supply clerks and supply officers. These people have a defined career path within which they receive all of their rewards and promotions for being able to maintain control of the assets within their areas of responsibility. There is also a strong requirement that the commander of a unit be responsible for the physical assets. In order for this approach to be effective in business, accomplishment or failure must be noted in the reward system of the company. Most managers are well aware that things get lost. Over their careers, they have watched the annual inventories and write ups and write downs with some amusement, but little concern.

Changing this attitude is a necessary ingredient to protection of assets. It is necessary to establish the responsibility of each manager. The custodian I.D. within the property record file allows for recording that identification. However, identification alone is not sufficient. The association of assets with the manager responsible for their custody must include some accountability on the part of the manager. He or she must be integrally involved with tracking and maintenance on a daily basis, not once a year at inventory time. Each manager should periodically receive reports that identify the assets assigned to him or her. Further, both past maintenance expense and forecasted maintenance expense by asset should be supplied. There also needs to be a simple way for the manager to report discrepancies. If a manager receives a maintenance report including a machine that has been transferred or sold, he or she should promptly notify the property accountant of that discrepancy. A manager close to the asset should be made responsible: a foreman can manage all of the equipment used by the crew or an office manager can supervise all of the furniture and fixtures within an office. Summary reports should also be available to bring to the attention of supervising managers the total assets within their organization.

In the military commander approach to asset management, the transfer of any manager requires the new manager to accept responsibility for all of the assets within their subordinate units. This by no means eliminates problems on reconciliation, but it reduces the attitude of "Have a team inventory once a year, get as close as they can to reconciliation, and forget it."

Emphasis on quality is being made by most companies today. A quality product placed in the customer's hands requires quality production equipment. Quality attitude should also prevail regarding the records of assets and the quality of maintenance that occurs. The amount of downtime on any given production equipment should be of concern to each manager. It will take effort to introduce this kind of process, which stresses maintaining property records and keeping a record of the performance and maintenance on each piece of equipment. The rewards will come in future years rather than in the current quarter.

It is important to recognize that 100 percent proficiency is unrealistic: a principle of expending a 90 percent effort to control 90 percent of capital dollars should prevail. The minimum capitalization level of at least $1,000 (but preferably $5,000) makes it possible to "sacrifice" the 10 percent that is bound to be lost.

The manager should also consider which assets need to be subject to tight controls. Is typical office furniture even worth the effort? It is not likely to be. Most organizations will expense the office furniture as purchased. Except when an organization shrinks and has excess furniture, it is going to be obvious if a chair or desk disappears. Most offices will be supplied with the number of chairs necessary and movement from one office to the other isn't an important factor to monitor. Perhaps individual assets of furniture greater than $5,000 are worth the effort to track and maintain. A key element in establishing the capitalization policy and the items to track and reconciling the actual record with the physical inventory is whether or not their loss would be critical to the organization. Production machinery that affects product quality can be critical. Similarly, equipment breakdowns that would idle the production line or a number of employees could be critical. These items need to be included in the highest priority of management.

FOREIGN CORRUPT PRACTICES ACT

The Foreign Corrupt Practices Act (FCPA) requires that companies subject to securities and exchange commission regulations maintain their books, records, and accounts each in reasonable detail. The records must also be accurate, and fairly reflect the transactions and dispositions of the company's assets. The Act spells out that companies must devise and maintain a system of internal accounting controls sufficient to provide reasonable assurance that the following objectives are met:

1. Transactions are executed in accordance with management's general or specific authorization
2. Transactions are recorded as necessary to permit preparation of financial statements in conformity with GAAP and maintain accountability for assets

3. Access to assets is permitted only in accordance with management's general and/or specific authorization

4. The recorded accountability of assets is compared with the existing assets at reasonable intervals and appropriate action is taken with respect to any discrepancies

This details a requirement to verify actual existence of assets. However, it is reasonable to verify the major assets and not necessarily all of the lesser ones. This can also be accomplished through a sample inventory technique and does not require a 100 percent physical inventory. The requirements of the FCPA are also met using the periodic verification in the "military commander" approach to asset custodian changes.

FULLY DEPRECIATED ASSETS

Accounting principles, the laws, and audit standards do not require that records be maintained of assets that have no value represented on the balance sheet. However, equipment which has lived longer than its estimated expected life may well be appropriate to maintain on the property record from a management standpoint.

Large aircraft, for example, are typically initially purchased by major airlines. Ford Trimotors of the 1930s were operated by the primary airlines of the time. A number of those aircraft are still operating in small countries today. An aircraft frequently lives beyond its original fifteen- or twenty-year depreciation life because of continuous maintenance programs. These items should be maintained on the property record. At the other extreme are items such as the office furniture of an executive. They may receive little wear and tear and actually be more valuable twenty years after purchase. Some attorney firms may still have the original bookshelves with the glass doors popular one hundred years ago. These need not be maintained on the property record. However, each company should review specifically and make a policy determination of what the criteria is for items that have been fully depreciated, but are still in use. The deciding criteria will be the need for management attention. In the case of an aircraft, it may still have significant market value. Replacement cost is likely to be covered by insurance. If insurance coverage due to fire or theft includes the asset, then it should be maintained on the property record and the fact of its physical existence should be verified on some basis. This does not require that every individual item be maintained, however. In the case of office furniture, a record of "four executive offices with furniture" may be the only record required. When an insurance claim is to be filed as a result of either fire or theft, it is necessary to provide proof of existence and subsequent loss. The property record can be an important source of proof.

Also, at insurance policy negotiation time, it is necessary to establish the amount of asset value in order to establish premiums. The property record can be important in providing this information.

REPORTS FROM THE PROPERTY RECORD SYSTEM

The information that has been recorded in the property record database will allow a number of reports to management to be created. The following are reports which will be created on a regular monthly, quarterly, and annual basis. Other reports may be requested.

Forecast reports
    Maintenance
    Asset replacement
    Vehicle registration
    Insurance value review
Management reports
    Maintenance cost per hour of use
    Hours of maintenance
    Unscheduled downtime due to maintenance problem
    Planned scheduled maintenance
    Production rate (units per hour)
    Location of equipment, responsibility for
    Movement of equipment
Property responsibility by manager

13

COMPUTER PROGRAMS

INTRODUCTION

As personal computers increase in capabilities and decrease in cost, more accounting detail can be kept in an easily accessible format. More employees are also becoming knowledgeable with computers. Not only are almost all college students using computers, but a large segment of elementary students are also. The typical accountant of today is as knowledgeable about computer accounting applications as a data-processing expert of the 1960s.

ASSET DATA BASE SOFTWARE

The additional software capabilities and reduced hardware costs allow maintenance of more data in a usable format. The problem in establishing any asset management system is ensuring that the amount of information kept is truly useful. It is possible with computers to store vast amounts of data. Data in and of itself, however, is not useful. It must be organized so that it provides information that is useful at the time needed. The database is analogous to a library that contains thousands of books. When one needs a specific book, there has to be organization to allow the library user to find it quickly. The same is true of a computer database: it must be organized in a way that the information required can be retrieved quickly out of the thousands, or perhaps millions, of pieces of data.

Accountants are being criticized for maintaining cost accounting information that does not supply the needed answers quickly. A detailed system that maintains vast amounts of data and summarizes it, but does not have the flexibility to respond to changed conditions is ultimately of little help. In developing an asset database, it is important to keep in mind simplicity and usability.

Asset accounting has not had a high priority in past system developments. Because of the lack of interest on the part of managers and accountants in managing assets, data processors have not invested time and energy in systems. Most of the efforts in past asset accounting packages have been produced to provide for the tax depreciation and investment tax credit calculations. The databases were very narrow, and were defined by the information and processes needed to produce the tax returns.

Substantial increases in asset investments have increased interest in their management. Also, the impact of large numbers of assets requiring replacement all at the same time has heightened the interest in being able to forecast and monitor deferred maintenance.

Within the regulatory accounting standard setting bodies, considerable effort is being expended in defining the rules for accounting and controlling assets. Because of this increased interest, a good deal of effort is being expended by both accounting and data processing companies. They are working hard now to catch up with asset management packages to meet industry needs. The developments in computer hardware are occurring much more rapidly than the software for asset management, however. The data processing companies are expending major efforts to convince customers that they have the complete, integrated asset management package. Although great strides have been made recently, there still is much more to be done to produce an integrated asset management system.

EXISTING DATA BASE PROGRAMS

There is a large selection of off-the-shelf preprogrammed asset database managers for personal computers. Although more than forty of these packages are advertised in the popular accounting and data processing magazines, none of them will provide for all of a particular company's property record needs. Therefore, it is necessary to review and choose the one that meets the majority of the company's needs or have a program written specifically. Programmers are available to provide a package tailored to the specific needs of the business, however this is a very expensive approach as well as time consuming. Also, it is still not likely to meet every need. The specially written program will only include those functions identified during the definition and design phases. The available packages in total contain most processes necessary. Reviewing and testing available asset manager programs against stated objectives needed to meet the company's needs is a good learning and identification step.

SOFTWARE SELECTION

The first step in any software decision is to define the system needed.

Definition is describing in general terms what is required of the database management system. Other chapters have described database content, desirable report outputs, and processes for providing updates to the asset manager. In a definition of the system, consider these processes: What content is desired in the database? Are all of those suggested required? Are past maintenance expenses needed for all assets by year, or in total? Is a record of state inspections for motor vehicles required? Having defined generally the contents needed in the database, review the method for updating. Will it be a separate stand-alone database or will it be integrated with the general ledger accounting system? If it will stand alone, an input document to be prepared by the purchasing or receiving departments to record the initial information for a creation of a property record should be designed. The communication between the existing accounting software and the database must be reviewed and described, then the output reports that are needed. These include depreciation, custodian, maintenance, and others.

Having defined the inputs, the contents, and the outputs from the database manager, the processing that will be required on an on-demand monthly, quarterly, and annual basis can be determined. Also, if a predefined computer environment that the database will operate in exists, it should be designated. Any limitations on storage and processing need specifications should be noted.

Having identified the type of system needed, the next step is to review the software in the marketplace to determine which ones might be suitable.

OFF-THE-SHELF PROPERTY RECORD DATABASE PACKAGES

Review what is on the market before deciding on an approach. This should be done even if it is likely the company will need to develop its own database program. A review is an education. It will provide ideas for functions that might not otherwise be considered. Also, some of the off-the-shelf packages can be modified to meet specific needs. At least one database program that is part of a total accounting system supports a considerable amount of "after-market" software. There are consulting firms that install the system and provide add-on packages. For example, one system does not come with a maintenance record as part of the database package, however one of the after-market firms has written such a maintenance record, and it is available for purchase and addition.

Another firm offers a relational database package that is advertised as running on any system, from the smallest personal computer to a large mainframe system. The relational database process has a means of defining expandable records that can be associated with one another. That company will tailor the process to your needs.

REVIEW COPIES OF SOFTWARE

Most of the software vendors either have review copies or will allow you to use their software for sixty to ninety days with no commitment. This is a good way to review the capabilities of the software and become familiar with the program. Although there are more than forty identified in the market, it is quite time-consuming to actually obtain, review the documentation on, load, and test different property record systems. Therefore, make selections in advance and plan to review a maximum of three or four packages. Otherwise the amount of staff investment in learning the systems and trying them out will be quite expensive.

If an integrated accounting and property record system is required, choice will be limited significantly. Most of the systems are tailored to producing the depreciation portion of the property records. They all provide multiple files for federal, state, and book depreciation, which may each be different. However, there are only a few that have an integrated system. None was found that actually was fully integrated. Most software packages that advertise as being integrated with accounting software are limited to the passing of depreciation computations from the property record system to the general ledger process. One company providing a relational database advertises that it is fully integrated with an accounting process, however their package was not available for review.

Consider whether the existing accounting software package has asset managing capabilities. There is considerably more work in installing a complete accounting package than there is in simply providing for a new property record system. If the present accounting system has a property record database system, that should be the first package for review, assuming the present accounting package has been satisfactory.

Before ordering a software package for review, have a plan for its evaluation outlined. Also, ensure that you can devote adequate time for the staff to become familiar with it, test it, and provide a critical review. It would be best to be able to devote a week or two of full-time effort to this task, as learning a new package is more time-consuming when done as a part-time function. Also consider that there are firms who will perform this step for the company, including definition, review, and even installation if that is what is needed. Both accounting and data processing firms have consultant sections that provide these services.

EVALUATION OF SOFTWARE PACKAGES

Having identified requirements for a software package, contact three or four software firms that, from their advertising, look like they may meet the requirements. Keep in mind that those that do not respond may not have very good technical support for their software package. From the responses received, select one to begin reviewing.

It may also be helpful to attend one of the asset management seminars provided by a number of organizations. Both the American Management Association and the Institute on Management Accounting, as well as a number of accounting and data processing firms, have seminars at various locations around the United States. These seminars not only review the concepts of asset management, but typically review one or more computer systems. Also, the students at these seminars will typically have some experience with one or more of the software packages and can give the benefit of their informal evaluation.

When ordering a copy of the review package, keep in mind that the initial cost of the system should not be the determining factor. Much more staff time will be spent in setting up the system than the cost of the package if it is an inferior product or unsuitable to the company's needs. And the availability of future maintenance updates are very important. The cost difference between these packages may be surprising. They range from $150 to $900, and the price itself is not indicative of the features that it provides. The one that is the most expensive does not have the most features.

Before the first review package arrives, be sure there is a written plan for evaluating the package.

PROGRAM REVIEW

Setup

What are the complexities? Is it simple to load with checklist instructions provided? The forethought that the programmers have provided for a simple loading on the system gives a good insight into their thinking and the complexities that will be presented in adding and changing records later.

What are the requirements for disk and computing resources? Make a record of how much it takes so that comparisons with other programs can be made. With the reduction in cost of memory and processing within personal computers, this is not a critical factor, however the amount of space provides an idea of what the program's capabilities are.

What staff support is available? And if any questions arose while loading, was that staff support available? Of four systems tested, all advertised staff support: two loaded with ease and no assistance was required; a problem was encountered on one that exceeded the disk space available, though it was well within the limits set forth within the documentation. Further investigation with assistance from staff, provided a week later, indicated that a recent modification to the program had increased its disk storage requirements. The staff support by phone eventually proved adequate, however a week's response time is not the best situation. What happens if, during monthly close activities, the program fails? Any indication of a problem with staff support should be documented and weighed carefully when making a final selection.

Integrated with Total Accounting System

Is the property record system integrated with a general ledger system? Is a new asset record established from the purchasing document? Test to be sure that the claim of integration is not just the passing of depreciation computations into the general ledger expense accounts. Rather, does the general ledger recording of a retirement or sale transaction update the asset record? A truly integrated system will provide the means for one entry to record a retirement or sale in both the general ledger and the asset management package.

Ease of Update

To update property records, is a pre-printed form provided? Is the document designed so that keying update information is easy? And are there input prompts? When a new record is keyed, the program should ideally provide for the fields to be displayed and would prompt their input. Similarly, there should be edits provided to verify the information as it is entered. The introduction of an incorrect general ledger account, asset class or category code, or location code can cause great difficulty once in the system. However, if those codes are compared to a valid list, at least the code entered is valid. Keying transcriptions will generally be caught at that point. Are there default codes for location, asset category, and classification as well as custodian? If a number of records are being updated, it is possible for the programmer to provide either the most common default placed in the record each time, or alternatively, or perhaps in addition, the value that was placed in the prior record. That way if a number of new assets that all have the same custodian are entered, it is only necessary to validate the default value that is already in the record. This saves considerable keystrokes and over the life of the system will both reduce time correcting errors and the time keying.

Edits should be provided to ensure that all required information is entered. Also, "reasonableness" values can be checked. Dates should be within the current year or send a flag; dollar amounts can be checked for reasonable values of no less than $100 and no more than the cost of the most expensive asset you have. It should also be possible to duplicate the entire previous record to reduce keying. This will reduce keying when a group of assets is purchased, such as furniture or automobiles. If all of the information is the same except the asset I.D. and serial numbers, then by duplicating the first record, only asset I.D. and serial number need be keyed for subsequent assets.

There should be a means to correct any misinformation at a later date. Some software packages make it difficult to change the information in the asset record without moving the entire item and replacing it. This is an opportunity for keying errors, as well as an additional effort.

An important update procedure should involve a report producing a turnaround document. This is a report produced by the computer listing all of the assets and the information involving them. When sent to the custodian for verification on the change of custodian or responsible manager, they are marked with the changes and returned to the computer operator. Only the changes need then be keyed into the system. This turnaround document is produced by the computer, modified by the custodian, and then used to update the database.

Database Flexibility

Does the package allow for sufficient coding? Is the length of the fields sufficient? In addition to the described fields, are there others available for user definition? There will be requirements for additional information for some assets. Although the database may not specifically provide for total maintenance expense or next required inspection of a motor vehicle, a flexible system will allow use of a user-defined field.

Standard Reports

Are there standard reports produced? These should be both calendar- and event-driven. Purchase of a new asset should send a report to the department custodian for verification of its receipt. Passing of a date of a required inspection should send notification to the custodian to ensure that it is done. Standard reports should also be easily supplemented with user-defined reports. Are reports produced monthly, quarterly, and annually? A system that produces standard reports which can be modified by the user is a significant benefit. There are other ways to provide for reports through spreadsheets and report generator packages, however, predefined reports can save considerable effort.

Review Report

When a software package is reviewed, notes should be made on a pre-designed form outlining the above concerns. Also, just jotting down a list of questions, problems, and experiences as they occur provides a good record for comparison between the two or three systems that are reviewed. After reviewing two or three, memory is not a good way to distinguish between them.

Following is a checklist that may be used as a starting point. There will, of course, be special requirements for each unique situation, which will need to be added.

CHECKLIST FOR PROGRAM REVIEW

Setup

    Complexity

    Disk space requirements

    Computer requirements

    Staff support availability and responsiveness, if required

Integration with total accounting system

    Depreciation calculations are not the only functions performed

    Purchase or payment document creates an asset record

    Retirement or sale transaction updates asset record

Ease of update

    Input prompts

    Default codes for location, asset category, class, custodian, edits for required information and reasonable values

    Dates, values, lives

    Previous record duplication

    Means to change incorrect information later

    Update procedure from a turnaround document

Database flexibility

    Identification codes, sufficient number and length

    Allowance for all data needed

    User-defined fields

Standard reports

    New adds for custodian

    On-demand and calendar-driven

User-defined reports

    Easy to define

    On-demand and calendar-driven

DATA BASE FIELDS

The following are examples only, each organization will have others.

Asset I.D. tag number
Physical location
Organization code
Custodian
General ledger account code
Description
    Description code—standard descriptions in asset manual
Date of acquisition
Original cost
Vendor
Estimated salvage value
Estimated economic life
Depreciation methods
    Fit, state, book, etc.
Cost of reproduction
Insurance coverage
Maintenance expense record, by years
Estimated deferred maintenance
Leased property
Expensed item

BIBLIOGRAPHY

GENERAL

Accounting for Foreclosed Assets, Statement of Position 92–93. Accounting Standards Division, American Institute of Certified Public Accountants: New York, 1992.

Corporate Valuation, A Business and Professional Guide. Gordon V. Smith. John Wiley & Sons, Inc.: New York, 1988.

Design and Maintenance of Accounting Manuals. Harry L. Brown. John Wiley & Sons, Inc.: New York, 1988.

Impairments and Write Offs of Long-Lived Assets. Dove Fried. National Association of Accountants: Montvale, New Jersey, 1989.

Reporting, Control, and Analysis of Property, Plant, and Equipment. Michael J. Sandretto. National Association of Accountants: Montvale, New Jersey, 1990.

Statements on Management Accounting 4J, Accounting for Property, Plant, and Equipment. Institute of Management Accountants: Montvale, New Jersey, 1989.

_____, *4L, Control of Property, Plant, and Equipment.* Institute of Management Accountants, Montvale, New Jersey, 1990.

_____, *Statement No. 4, Fixed Asset Accounting: The Capitalization of Costs.* National Association of Accountants: Montvale, New Jersey, 1972.

Reinventing the Corporation. John Naisbitt. Warner Books: Inc., New York, 1985.

FINANCIAL ACCOUNTING STANDARDS FOR BUSINESS

FASB Statement 2, Accounting for Research and Development Costs. Financial Accounting Standards Board: Stamford, Connecticut, 1974.

FASB Statement 32, Specialized Accounting and Reporting Principles and Practices in AICPA Statements of Position and Guides on Accounting and Accounting Matters, Financial Accounting Standards Board: Stamford, Connecticut, 1979.

FASB Statement 34, Capitalization of Interest Cost. Financial Accounting Standards Board: Stamford, Connecticut, 1979.

FASB Statement 42, Determining Materiality for Capitalization of Interest Cost. Financial Accounting Standards Board: Stamford, Connecticut, 1980.

FASB Statement 71, Accounting for Affects of Certain Types of Regulation. Financial Accounting Standards Board: Stamford, Connecticut, 1982.

FASB Statement 90, Regulated Enterprises—Accounting for Abandonments and Disallowances of Plant Costs. Financial Accounting Standards Board: Stamford, Connecticut, 1986.

FASB Statement 92, Regulated Enterprises—Accounting for Phase in Plans. Financial Accounting Standards Board: Stamford, Connecticut, 1987.

FASB Statement 93, Recognition of Depreciation by Not-for-Profit Organizations. Financial Accounting Standards Board: Stamford, Connecticut, 1987.

FASB Statement 99, Deferral of Effective Date of Recognition of Depreciation by Not-for-Profit Organizations—An Amendment of FASB Statement 93. Financial Accounting Standards Board: Stamford, Connecticut, 1988.

FASB Statement 101, Regulated Enterprises—Accounting for Discontinuation of Application of FASB Statement 71. Financial Accounting Standards Board: Stamford, Connecticut, 1988.

GAAP Interpretation and Application of Generally Accepted Accounting Principles, 1992 Edition. Patrick R. Delany. John Wiley & Sons, Inc.: New York.

International Accounting Standard Exposure Draft 43, Proposed Statement—Property, Plant, and Equipment. International Accounting Standards Committee: London, England, May 1992.

Financial Accounting Series No. 098 B, Discussion Memorandum, Accounting for the Impairment of Long-Lived Assets and Identifiable Intangibles. Financial Accounting Standards Board: Stamford, Connecticut, 1990.

ACCOUNTING FOR NOT-FOR-PROFIT ORGANIZATIONS

Audits of Providers of Health Care Services. American Institute of Certified Public Accountants: New York, 1989.

Financial and Accounting Guide for Not-for-Profit Organizations, Fourth Edition. Malvern J. Gross, Jr. John Wiley & Sons, Inc.: New York, 1991.

Exposure Draft Proposed FAS 96-B, Accounting for Contributions Received and Contributions Made and Capitalization of Works of Art, Historical Treasures, and Similar Assets. Financial Accounting Standards Board: Stamford, Connecticut, 1990.

FAS 120-B Exposure Draft, Financial Statements of Non-Profit Organizations. Financial Accounting Standards Board: Stamford, Connecticut, 1992.

GOVERNMENT ACCOUNTING

GAS 14, The Financial Reporting Entity. Government Accounting Standards Board: Norwalk, Connecticut, 1991.

Government Fixed Asset Inventory Systems, Establishing, Maintaining, and Accounting. Paul E. Glick. Government Finance Officers Association: Chicago, Illinois, 1987.

Governmental Accounting, Auditing and Financial Reporting. Government Finance Officers Association: Chicago, Illinois, 1988.

Governmental Accounting and Financial Reporting Standards, Section 1400-Fixed Assets. Government Accounting Standards Board: Norwalk, Connecticut, 1992.

Private Sector Performance Measures and Their Applicability to Government Operations. David J. Harr. National Association of Accountants: Montvale, New Jersey, 1991.

Reinventing Government. David Osborne. Addison-Wesley Publishing Company, Inc.: Reading, Massachusetts, 1992.

REGULATED INDUSTRIES

Cost Accounting Standards Board; Recodification of Cost Accounting Standards Board Rules and Regulations, Code Federal Regulations, 48 CFR Parts 9900-9904. Government Printing Office: Washington, D.C., 1992.

Railroad Accounting Principles. Railroad Accounting Principles Board: Washington, D.C., 1987.

Telecommunication—Code of Federal Regulations, 47 CFR Part 32 Uniform System of Accounts for Telecommunications Companies. Office of the Federal Register, National Archives and Records Administration: Washington, D.C., 1992.

_____ *Part 34, Uniform System of Accounts for Radio Telegraph Carriers.* Office of the Federal Register, National Archives and Records Administration: Washington, D.C., 1992.

_____ *Part 35, Uniform System of Accounts for Wire, Telegraph and Ocean Cable Carriers.* Office of the Federal Register, National Archives and Records Administration: Washington, D.C., 1992.

_____ *Part 36, Jurisdictional Separations Procedures; Standard Procedures for Separating Telecommunications Property Costs, Revenues, Expenses, Taxes, and Reserves for Telecommunications Companies.* Office of the Federal Register, National Archives and Records Administration: Washington, D.C., 1992.

Transportation, CFR 49, Part 1200 General Accounting Regulations Under the Interstate Commerce Act. Office of the Federal Register, National Archives and Records Administration: Washington, D.C.

INDEX